Anointing
of
Motherhood

FAST, PRAY AND STUDY ABOUT CARING FOR
GOD'S PRECIOUS LITTLE ONES

SHEREENA MONIQUE OSAI (LILY)

To my husband, Esosa Osai: This thing with us is deep like the ocean…we intersect in so many ways, there is no separating where one ends and the other begins. We are one. Your encouragement, wisdom and vision, faith and hard work has helped shape me into the mother I am. You are God's gift to the children and I.

To my children, it is my desire to be all that Yahuah has designed me to be in your life. Through the power of God, I want you to be rooted and grounded in Christ, ready to give an answer for the hope that lives inside of you and prepared for every good work God has for you. Thank you for your love. You all have my heart.

To my mother, Doreen who is in heaven now, but her work in my life still lives. I am grateful for all you taught me, all of the encouragement and most importantly for leading me to Christ and helping disciple me. Your prophetic insight helped guide me to the family my Heavenly Father had planned for me. There are no words to express how thankful I am.

To my father, Hilton Kelley: Thank you for all the wisdom you have shared with me, the love you have shown me and for always being there for me. I am so thankful to have you in my life. You have been a great encouragement.

To my Heavenly Father: You are my Shepherd, your name is my refuge and without you I can do nothing. Thank you for never giving up on me, thank you for your mercy, love and correction. Thank you for giving your son Yeshua (Jesus Christ) to die on the cross for my sins and for making me brand new. ***There is no greater love.***

Contents

Preface

On Saturday, December 4, 2010 at 11:15 a.m, my son Champion was born and I became a mother. After twelve hours of laboring through the night, pain and contractions, and countless pushes, my son finally laid in my arms. His eyes were beautiful and calming. When I saw his face, the distress of the past twelve hours melted away. I was a mother. My connection with him felt so strong. As soon as he was laid in my arms, I felt that I instinctively knew what he needed. I was smitten.

After having my son, I developed this urge to connect with other moms; to surround myself with women. I needed their stories, advice, remedies, jokes, and to connect with women walking the journey.

Having a community of women around you as you learn and grow can be so valuable. Playdates, book clubs, bible studies, and meeting strangers at the park that became close friends were all ways that I was able to glean from other women and feed that hunger for connectivity that raising children created in me.

During the first year of motherhood, I felt like I was discovering secrets about my own mother, finding answers to questions that always puzzled me. As I got up through the night to feed my son, going without sleep for days to care for him, and putting my to-do list on the backburner to give him the care he needed, I felt I was finally discovering the sacrifice it took to raise my sisters and I.

Mothers are gifted by God to nurture and meet the physical needs of their children. But a mother's love can go even deeper by reaching into the spirit realm. When you are a mother and a follower of Christ, God can use you to not only nurture your child physically, but to disciple, lead, and guide them spiritually. God can pour on you an anointing to mother your children both naturally and spiritually. What a powerful combination.

My mother gave everything she had. She gave everything she did not have. Always trying to give us more than what she had growing up. She always said that each generation should be better than the one before and she did her best to live that. She definitely struggled through motherhood and made lots of mistakes, but I knew she loved us and was grateful for that.

As children, we got to witness her complete transformation from a life of clubbing, smoking and drinking, to receiving salvation through Jesus Christ. What a wonderful transformation it was. Our lives drastically changed for the better. The light of Christ Jesus truly does shine bright, piercing through gross darkness.

Because my mother gave her life to Christ, I was able to hear the gospel and make a decision to follow Christ as well. Now that I am a mother, I am able to teach my children about the Savior as well. Giving them what my mother gave me: discipleship in Christ. This is the greatest gift a mother can give her children. How blessed to give birth to a child, then lead them to rebirth in Christ Jesus! For Jesus said, you must be born again.

This is my greatest joy as a mother, leading my children to their heavenly Father, their creator, and the One that promises to never leave them. So far, Yahuah has touched all of our children's hearts and they have all asked to receive salvation through Jesus Christ by the time they were two years old. It came by prayer, reading and explaining the Bible to them daily, having discussions, and teaching them right from wrong based on God's living word. I have no greater joy than to hear that my children walk in truth (3 John 1:4).

For me, becoming a mother created a need in my life for my mother on a different level. As I mentioned before, I gained a greater understanding of my mom after giving birth. But I also felt a need to just connect with and learn from her.

I spent so much of my adolescence thinking my mom was nuts. Now, I realized what I thought was her craziness, was really her motherly insight and intuition. In my youth, I needed that at more than I ever knew. When I became a mom, I needed to cultivate that in myself.

Sometimes, I needed advice from my mom about motherhood or about my marriage. When I called her, she was an empathic listening ear. Other times, she would give me the word of God on the matter and set me straight. It seems she took this charge to heart: "That they may teach the young women to be sober, to love their husbands, to love their children, to be discreet, chaste, keepers at home, good, obedient to their own husbands, that the word of God be not blasphemed" (Titus 2:4–5).

My mother had such a hand in Yahuah bringing my family into being. God really used her. She moved to Michigan from our home in California when I was a senior in high school. I thought she was crazy. Then God told me to follow her to Michigan one year later. We lived in Kalamazoo, Michigan and I started college there. A few years later, my mother moved to Detroit; I thought she was totally crazy to move there. God has the last say and told me to follow her to Detroit one or two years later. God brought my husband and I soon after I moved to Detroit. Turns out my mother wasn't crazy, but led by the Holy Spirit. She was literally like Ruth, leading me to God's plans for me. I could not be more grateful.

Just as my mother's strengths have left an indelible mark in my life, so do her shortcomings. A lot of the struggles I faced in motherhood were due to the things my mother lacked or things she never conquered. My mother suffered abuse at the hands of her mother, which affected her and her siblings greatly. She did a lot better than her mom when raising us, but there was still an unhealthy level of verbal and physical abuse my sisters and I were subjected to growing up. These are the things that God has been dealing with in me, healing me, rebuking, and correcting me so the cycle of generational abuse can be stopped. I work through, pray through, and overcome these things to be the mother Yahuah is calling me to be, and bear the Godly seed that He is calling me to bear.

God has called me to be a wife and a mother. I tried to be other things and do other things while being a wife and mom. However, Yahuah keeps bringing me back to this as if to say, "focus". I wanted to be a fashion designer, interior designer, fashion stylist; the list goes on. But after God told me to let go of those goals, I had an epiphany.

God never told me I would be any of those things. He told me was that I would be a wife and a mother. And that is what I am.

Through all of this, God has taught me so much and has been forming His character, witness, and perseverance inside of me. I hope to share that with you to encourage you and build you up as you walk your own journey of motherhood. God is definitely not done with me and is completing the work He started in me. It is my joy to share with you what I have learned.

This book is a mix of things that God has taught me in His word or spoken to me by the Spirit, things other women have shared with me, things my mother taught me, and things I have observed as I labor in my home with my family. I pray that as you read, God would speak to you in a unique and powerful way.

This book is for mothers in every way the word can be defined. For the married, single, adopted moms, foster mothers, moms raising or providing support for children who have lost their mothers: this is for you. Being a mother takes so much courage and requires such a sacrifice of yourself. I hope that this information can help give you encouragement to keep going when you are weary, persevere when days are hard, and thrive in your role as you raise up the next generation.

FASTING AND PRAYING FOR THE ANOINTING OF MOTHERHOOD

> **Mark 9:**[28] And when he was come into the house, his disciples asked him privately, Why could not we cast him out?
> [29] And he said unto them, This kind can come forth by nothing, but by prayer and fasting

> **Matthew 9:**[14] Then came to him the disciples of John, saying, Why do we and the Pharisees fast oft, but thy disciples fast not?
> [15] And Jesus said unto them, Can the children of the bridechamber mourn, as long as the

bridegroom is with them? but the days will come, when the bridegroom shall be taken from them, and then shall they fast

Daniel 10:[12] Then said he unto me, Fear not, Daniel: for from the first day that thou didst set thine heart to understand, and to chasten thyself before thy God, thy words were heard, and I am come for thy words.

Fasting is an amazing spiritual tool that sets your heart to seek God, moves God, and brings deliverance and breakthrough like nothing else can! All the major victories in my life with Christ come by prayer and fasting. ALL OF THEM! Even Christ himself (God in the flesh, without sin) fasted.

When I was in high school, the Lord gave me a warning, revealing that if He were to come back, I was not ready and that I was not right with Him. Growing up in deliverance ministries, I knew I had a lot of demonic strongholds that needed to be broken. So, I fasted. It was so long ago now I cannot remember the specifics of the fast, but I know it included no television, no secular music (which I knew was demonic), and praying and reading the Bible in my room after school. I cannot remember the food aspect of the fast or the duration. But after that fast, I was NEVER the same.

One night during the fast, I was in my room listening to gospel music; I was getting tired of the music honestly. I could feel the demons/darkness inside me squirming. I turned the music up louder and began to sing, pray, and cry out to God. Tears began to flow down my face like a river and I began vomiting. I experienced great deliverance that night. That fast broke demonic strong holds in my life and I was able to grow and develop in my relationship with Christ.

Fast forward to college, I knew I needed deliverance again. I fasted and God opened my eyes spiritually to see some of the things I was doing that kept me bound, namely the entertainment I allowed into my heart and my life.

More recently, my family and I have started doing Daniel fasts yearly, including our children. During these fasts, we have experienced angelic visitation, dreams of God's throne in heaven, financial breakthrough, and spiritual revelation.

Going through this devotional while fasting simultaneously will bring a level of power and deliverance that cannot be obtained any other way. Not because of the book, but because God said that some deliverances we need can ONLY happen when we fast and pray.

I know for myself there are many personal issues that can creep up and hinder me as I minister to my children: selfishness, pride, fear, anger, anxiety, and doubt. There is no better way to get in the presence of God to petition Him for your deliverance than to fast. Reading the devotional in your fast will help you focus on specific things to pray for, key scriptures, and topics to meditate on for growth.

There are different ways to fast:

- No food for a designated period
- No food, no water for a designated period
- Fasting from one meal a day for a set period (example, skipping lunch for 40 days)
- Fasting one day per week for a set period (example, fasting all day Monday for 4 weeks)
- Daniel fast, no meat, sweets, or breads. Only eating fruit, veggies, nuts, beans for 21 days
- Cutting off entertainment/social indulgences (television, social media, excessive talking on the phone, etc.) to focus on the word and prayer

Either way you choose to fast, the goal is to set aside space in your life to seek God on a more focused and intense level. I encourage 40 days to coincide with the completion of the devotional. But you can fast however long you feel God leading you and continue through the book even if you fast for a shorter period of time.

Of course, fasting is NOT a requirement to read this book! However, I am compelled to share the tremendous impact that fasting can have when you are trying to grow spiritually at a moment in time of your life, or if you need great breakthrough or deliverance.

TIPS

If you have friends who are also mothers, it may be fun to go through the devotional and fast together. Having someone to talk with and pray through the topics with may help enrich the experience.

But if you do not have anyone to go through it with, I trust that you will still get what you need and Yah will walk with you.

Resist the urge to read ahead. The book is designed to give you food for thought to meditate, and really pray about. So read it one day at a time.

Read it with a journal to write down any thoughts, questions or ideas that may stir in your mind. This will help you chart personal applications and remember your thoughts down the line.

I pray that you would experience a life changing breakthrough from God's word as it relates to being a Godly mother. It is a high calling that changes the world.

Introduction

The realities of being a mother were much different than I thought. The demand of a new baby quickly revealed many character flaws I did not know I had. The demands change as the baby grows into a toddler, toddler to pre-school, etc. I found with each new phase of motherhood I was lacking some skill set or trait of godliness that would benefit me, my child, and our family as a whole.

What to do? Prayer? Yes. But I yearned to have connections with godly women to inspire, encourage, and help me learn! I had my mom, she was awesome, and Yahuah had placed other godly women in my life to fill that need. But I still found myself wishing I had been better prepared for this journey.

As we had more and more children, most older women, even in church, would give sly remarks about me having too many, or they were glad it was me and not them, or they were glad their children were grown and gone. Though most were only poking fun and making jokes, to me they revealed underlying issues with how we view children and childbearing.

There was simply a lack of older women willing to fulfill the role of teacher to younger women, teaching them to love their husbands and children. I have discussed this issue with a few women my age who agree. There are some women willing to do that job and take that role, but we need more.

Although my head is not yet white with the wisdom of the aged, I am here to be a voice and share what I know with you. To share what the Most High has taught me this far in hopes that I can encourage you where you are in your journey of motherhood.

Motherhood can uncover insecurities, character flaws, needs, desires, failures, hurts, and traumas. Many women have suffered terrible things in their childhood, relationship, marriage that greatly affect how they mother their children.

We as women are often in need of healing, deliverance, discipleship, and the love of God to fully be able to give what is required of us as mothers. When you become a mother, you do not instantly become a perfect person with all the answers. There can be so many layers that must be peeled back to uncover our potential to love, give, and serve our children and families.

In this concise, daily devotional I hope you will find some tools to help you overcome, and peel back some of those layers, with God, all things are possible (Matthew 19:26). The healing, transformation, strength, encouragement, and anointing you need to be a good mother is in God. If you follow Him, He promises to never leave you, and when you are weak, that's when He is strong.

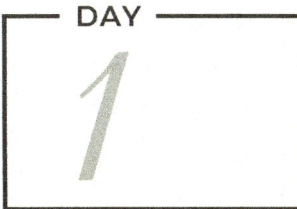
Do You Really Want This Blessing?

If you want to be married, then you want to be a mother.

My husband always had the idea that you should not date until you were ready to get married, and you should not get married until you are ready to have children.

Why start a romantic relationship and then realize you are not in a position in life to be married? It can cause heartbreak and frustration. Why get married and then tell your spouse, let's put off having children? Then all sorts of unnatural and ungodly measures must be taken to avoid pregnancy.

If you are married at a young age, it is naturally the season of life for bearing children. It is the natural progression and the natural next step. For a woman, being able to have children is a window of opportunity that does not last forever.

I have met countless elderly women who told me they regretted not having children, or that they regretted having only a few, they wished they had had more. Their mature mind can now see what their young mind did not believe: children are a blessing.

It is best to follow what the word of God says, even when people or our own emotions say otherwise.

I thought I really wanted the blessing of children. When I was sixteen, God showed me the blessing of my future children. I was at home mopping the floor and Yah spoke to me and told me that I was going to have many children. I would have many sons; the Lord told me the world needed my sons.

When He spoke this to me, I accepted His calling. I only asked that if it was His will, that I could have a least two daughters. This was in the year 2000.

When the Lord spoke to me so clearly, I was very excited. He put love in my heart for my children, and I loved them all immediately. The word was so real, although it would not come to pass for another ten years. The Lord led me to Psalm 127, it filled me with so much joy, confirming what God had spoken to me.

Psalm 127

³ Lo, children are an heritage of the Lord: and the fruit of the womb is his reward.
⁴ As arrows are in the hand of a mighty man; so are children of the youth.
⁵ Happy is the man that hath his quiver full of them: they shall not be ashamed, but they shall speak with the enemies in the gate.

Although I received this word with gladness and began confessing this and standing on the blessing of many children… the Word was tested.

After I had my first child, I felt like my life was over. The trauma of childbirth, the rush of emotional and hormonal changes, sleep deprivation, and post-partum depression had me on the ropes. Caring for a newborn for the first time was much more difficult than I had anticipated. I could not go out with my husband as much as I used to. I felt like I was trapped in the house forever.

I immediately decided that I did not want to have any more children. I was done. It took almost a year for God to get my mind together.

He worked on my heart, showed me my selfishness. He showed me how I was spoiled, and self-centered (children have the tendency to unearth hidden flaws in parents). Reading the bible, praying, and reading books about motherhood really helped encourage me. After a while, God once again renewed my original vision that He gave me when I was in high school: to allow God to fill my quiver.

Now I am on my eighth pregnancy and I'm so glad I did not succumb to my emotions but allowed God to mold my thoughts to His.

Malachi 2:15

And did not he make one? Yet had he the residue of the spirit. And wherefore one? That he might seek a godly seed. Therefore take heed to your spirit, and let none deal treacherously against the wife of his youth.

1 Timothy 2:15

Notwithstanding she shall be saved in childbearing, if they continue in faith and charity and holiness with sobriety.

What are your thoughts on having children?

If you already have children, what are your thoughts on allowing God to give you more if you are still able to have them?

Are these thoughts based on scripture? How can you grow and be transformed in your mind by God's word on this topic?

If you are unable to have more children, or are unable to have biological children, what are some ways you can present a Godly attitude about children to others?

How can you still bear Godly seed in other ways (discipleship, mentorship, adoption, foster parenting, volunteering with children, etc.)?

3

PRAYER

Abba Father, your word says that children are a heritage from you and a reward. Please help me and transform my mind to think the way you do about children. Help me to see them and the purpose you have given them. Please give me the strength, courage and love to produce Godly seed. In the name of your son Yeshua, Amen.

Build Your House

It's really the role of the woman to set the tone in the house.

As mothers, whether we want to face it or not; our attitudes, moods and temper affect the entire atmosphere of our homes. This was something my mother Doreen shared with me when I first became a mother. "It's really the role of the woman to set the tone in the house".

I did not want to believe her; I did not want the responsibility that seemed to come along with that statement. Believing what she said meant I would not be able to always say what I feel, respond how I want. As an emotionally expressive person, this was a sobering fact for me.

Learning to control my attitudes, emotions, and words would also force me to mature in much deeper ways. Thinking more deeply about building others and making that the central focus over my own expression and emotional release.

As women we have so many emotions, feelings, thoughts, and responsibilities. We are also constantly juggling the emotions, feelings, thoughts, and responsibilities of our husbands and children.

It can be hard to keep a calm and peaceful atmosphere in our own minds, let alone set a peaceful tone in our homes. Having peace in your home does not mean that there won't be hard days or difficult situations. What it means is that you make wise choices on how you handle those hard situations.

With my mother's wisdom in mind, I set out to attempt to curate a peaceful atmosphere in our house. To be honest I did not feel very successful, but I was trying every day, nonetheless.

One evening, I was giving my young daughter a bath; she was around two years old at the time. I was tired and felt very overwhelmed; it had been a hard day for me. My four-year-old son walked into the bathroom and handed me a dollar. I looked at him and asked what it was for. He said he wanted to give it to me because I am such a great mom. In that moment, every negative thought and emotion I had was shattered. This is what it is about and what I am doing all of this for, love. The fact that my son still felt love and was able to give love, despite all the negativity I felt inside, meant everything to me. It was a token that my attempts to love, my attempts to build up my family, to build my house were having an effect. My work bearing good fruit, my labor not all in vain. I hugged my son and thanked him. And I cried tears of joy.

Building our house means building the people that live in it. Building up their hearts with courage, their minds with wisdom, and their spirits with the word of God. Filling them with love. If we can focus in, zoom in and focus on building with these tools, and discipline our own emotions so as not to pick up the wrong tools and start tearing the house down, our families will be on the way to being and bearing the Godly seed Yahuah desires.

The Holy Spirit is a guide that leads us into all truth, the word lights our path, and Jesus' example is always there, lighting the path to humility. We can do all things through Christ who strengthens us.

So, I say to you woman of God: you can respond with peace in every situation, every time. You can lead by example in kindness, respectfulness, love and hope. Let your humility shine for all your family to see.

In the end, if humility is your goal. You will lower yourself before the Lord and operate in your home the way He desires in order to bear good fruit.

Anger, rage, lack of self-control, smart comments, and put downs are tools of darkness that will pluck your house down, not build it up.

Submit your emotions to God in prayer and ask Him to help you have the right response in every situation, so that your family will be cocooned in an atmosphere of peace.

Proverbs 14:1–3

Every wise woman buildeth her house: but the foolish plucketh it down with her hands.
   He that walketh in his uprightness feareth the Lord: but he that is perverse in his ways despiseth him.
   In the mouth of the foolish is a rod of pride: but the lips of the wise shall preserve them.

Proverbs 31:26

She openeth her mouth with wisdom; and in her tongue is the law of kindness.

Psalm 101:2

I will behave myself wisely in a perfect way. O when wilt thou come unto me? I will walk within my house with a perfect heart

PRAYER

Abba Father, please forgive me for the times I allowed my emotions to rule me and rob my family of peace.

God, please forgive me for times I have hurt my husband and children with angry responses instead of kindness. I ask for your grace, love and communion of your Spirit to be with me as I serve my family every day. In the name of your son Yeshua I pray. Amen

Note: Write down anything He speaks or brings to your remembrance or any ideas He gives you to have a more peaceful home moving forward.

Sensitivity to The Spirit Will Protect Your Family

*You have to take responsibility and look after
your family and children with diligence.*

As a mother, it is important to consider everything in your daily situations and understand that every decision has consequences that will bear fruit, whether good or bad.

When I was a child and into my adult life, many activities or plans that I had were interrupted by my mother's prophetic dreams or inclinations. Many times, I had plans that were changed or altered because God told my mother something; she had a dream, or just got a bad feeling.

Sometimes this would upset me, and other times I was in awe at her ability to see, sense, and discern in the spirit realm. Needless to say, I did not have a typical childhood.

My mother passed away in 2019, and things she told me before she died are still coming to pass. What a gift. I believe that God gives parents the ability to lead their children naturally and spiritually, if they will receive it, walk in the Spirit, and cease from the flesh.

As parents we are called to look after our families. That does not just mean housekeeping and making sure they get through school. It also means watching over them spiritually, relationally, emotionally.

LOOKING AFTER THEM SPIRITUALLY

This means discipling them into Christ-likeness. Not just depending on your church's Sunday school or youth group to do this work, but diligently teaching them the word of God, praying with and for them, and seeking God for direction for their lives.

Also, checking fruit is important. Are they bearing the fruits of the Spirit? Are they walking in love and kindness, are they speaking God's word and encouraging themselves and others? Some of these things take time and begin to show as the child matures.

The main thing is to be sure you are reading the Word to them, and with the grace of the Lord Jesus, modeling Christ-like character in front of them.

It is also important to fellowship with a body of believers that will encourage your children and the family's walk with Christ, not hindering it by breaking His Commandments.

LOOKING AFTER THEM EMOTIONALLY

Although you cannot cater to every whim and desire that your child has, it is important to have a strong emotional bond with your child. They should know that you care about how they feel, even if you cannot change certain decisions based on their feelings.

They should know how much you love them and be told verbally often. They should also be encouraged on a regular basis, especially in seasons when they are misbehaving and being disciplined often.

Cushions of love, affirmation, and encouragement should be surrounding your child at all times.

This might take some inner healing work on your part. Sometimes we are so wounded from difficulties in life or childhood trauma, that loving and encouraging words are hard for us to give.

Asking God to come in and heal those wounded places, allowing Him to take you on a journey of healing, will help open the spout of love so you can pour it over your children.

Also, some people have a hard time being verbally affectionate, however, your child still needs that from you. Practice speaking at least three encouraging and loving things per day, and it will become easier and easier.

LOOKING AFTER THEM RELATIONALLY

The importance of this cannot be overstated. Who your child interacts with can greatly impact their life, future, and the type of adult they become.

Moments with the right people shift your child's perspective and help steer them on the right path. Encounters with the wrong people can bring harm and detriment that can take a lifetime to heal.

I am not trying to scare anyone, just being totally honest and realistic. In an ideal world, everyone would be kind, encouraging and nurturing to children.

Unfortunately, this is not an ideal world, rather a fallen world that is greatly influenced by the prince of the power of the air (the devil) that is now in the earth.

However, those who have received salvation are now under the authority of Jesus Christ, which means we should be led by the spirit of God in all matters. If you pray and ask, God will begin to lead you on who your children should and should not spend time with. He will begin to give you warnings about certain people who pose danger, either spiritually or naturally. He will begin to teach you how to follow His voice.

Family members can be some of the most dangerous for children, therefore pray about what family to have your children around or not. Most sexual abuse children suffer is by the hands of family members.

Romans 8:14

They that are led by the Spirit of God are the sons of God.

Proverbs 3:6

In all thy ways acknowledge him, and he shall direct thy paths.

PRAYER

Abba Father, I thank you for my child/children and for the gift they are to my life. Lord, I pray that you would give me the wisdom, insight, and ability to look after them in every way.

God, ultimately you are the only one who can meet all their needs and be their guide and protector. But as their mother, please help me be and do all that I can to lead them in the way they should go. In the name of your son Yeshua I pray. Amen.

Be Strong with Gods Strength!

Don't shrink back! It's hard work; but with God,
you can strengthen yourself for the task.

Early mornings, late nights, colds and coughs, fevers, and sick nights, it all comes with the territory. The laundry piles up and the mail does, too.

Sometimes the to-do list increases and your energy and time decrease. How do you handle it all?

Currently, I am asking the same questions. How can I do all of this? I am pregnant with our eighth child. We are homeschooling and in the midst of a few small home repairs. Spring is upon us and there is a lot of work to do outside.

I have to work out consistently, keep me and my girl's hair washed, detangled, and styled regularly. I also cut my boys hair, not to mention normal housework and meal prep.

It can feel overwhelming, overpowering even. But what I am learning is that criticizing myself doesn't help. It just weakens my confidence. Complaining doesn't work; it just makes me cranky and a miserable wife and mother. Who wants to be around a cranky mommy or wife (Proverbs 21:9)?

So, what does work?

Strengthening yourself works. Don't shrink back! It's hard but with God, you can strengthen yourself for the task.

Encouraging yourself, celebrating your victories, and finding solutions to problems.

Strengthening yourself in the Spirit of God through prayer, fasting, worship, and reading God's word.

Exercising to decrease stress and improve energy.

Yes, strengthening yourself works!

Finding your strength in God to be a dynamic wife and mother takes a lot of prayer, but when you cry out—believe God will answer. Pray for power to implement every strategy that He shows you.

Also, reach out for help. Asking a friend to help you with laundry once a week or a grandparent to come over and play with the children while you do meal prep work. Also, asking your husband to pitch in on certain things when he is not working.

If you are able, hiring cleaning help is an option that may be more affordable than you think. Even if the hired help is just for a season, it could alleviate a lot a pressure until the children are older and can pitch in themselves a bit more.

Setting a schedule and getting certain things done before the children wake up is a big help. This one can be tricky when they are super young. When I had just babies and young toddlers, they would wake up early with me. Lol, fail!

Our logic with hired help is that it's best to hire help for the housework and cooking to free me up so I can devote more time to the children. My husband and I want me to invest as much time as possible into my children.

When things get hard and negative thoughts come, confess and speak out loud all the good things you KNOW to be true even if you don't feel it.

Children ARE a blessing.

You CAN do all things through Christ who strengthens you.

God's strength is made perfect in your weakness.

Proverbs 31:17

She girdeth her loins with strength, and strengtheneth her arms.

Philippians 4:13

I can do all things through Christ which strengtheneth me.

2 Corinthians 12:9

And he said unto me, My grace is sufficient for thee: for my strength is made perfect in weakness. Most gladly therefore will I rather glory in my infirmities, that the power of Christ may rest upon me.

PRAYER

Abba Father, I thank you. You are the giver of life. Thank you for the lives you have placed under my care. I thank you in advance for giving me the strength, wisdom and power to be an excellent mother in your kingdom.

Lord, you know my weaknesses, and I ask that you would strengthen those weak and broken places. Father, your word says that I can do all things through Christ who strengthens me. Make that my reality, help and empower me for this great work you have called me to in building my house. In the mighty name of your son Yeshua I pray. Amen.

Be Made Whole

Your Abba Father will restore any broken pieces of your heart.

Broken. I did not know I was broken. There has been so much healing from wounds, repenting from sins, and recovery from trauma that God has walked me through since having children. Having a person, or people who are totally dependent on you day and night, can uncover weaknesses and flaws like few things can. God began surfacing hurts and pains from my childhood when I went to college, but the healing ramped up after I got married, and ramped up even more after having children. Perhaps God wanted me to be healed so I can be a good wife and mom; perhaps situations that arose after marriage and children forced issues to the surface. I am not sure. What I do know is that God has performed many open-heart surgeries on me. Many times, I would have a dream or just be up in the night with memories playing in my mind. The tears would begin to fall, and I would begin to pray, and God would talk to me, comfort me and bring healing, forgiveness, comfort, whatever was needed. My husband helped to talk me through many of these episodes as well late into the night.

There are many ways God can heal us of hurts and pains from our past. Your emotional healing journey with Yahuah may look different than mine. But I can assure you, God is a healer. Other ways God has dealt with me and helped me heal, be delivered, or overcome is by showing me ungodly habits or character flaws and teaching me how to change them. For instance, yelling at my children. God showed me through a dream that this was evil, anger without cause, and was murderous (SCRIPTURE). He showed me that I was setting a bad example and that my yelling was influencing my children and how they treat each other.

> One night I dreamed that I was having a meeting with a prophetess in my room, the door was closed, and she and I were talking. Outside the door, my son was yelling at my other children. It was obvious to she and I that he got that from my example. In the dream, I was so embarrassed.

Another time I was praying, after having yelled at one of the boys for something. God spoke to me so clearly and told me I was a goat. I wasn't sure I heard him correctly and He said it again. "You are a goat". That was shocking to hear my God and master say those words to me. I meditated on what He said for weeks. Finally, I found the scripture that related to what He told me;, it was Matthew 25:31–46. In this passage Jesus is telling His disciples about what will happen when He returns. He told them that all nations would be gathered before Him and He will put His sheep on the right and the goats on the left. The goats are those who do not properly love and care for the very least of people; the sheep are those that do. When we care for the least, we are caring for Christ himself, when we do not, we are neglecting Christ Himself. How does that relate to what Yahuah calling me a goat? Well, children are like the least in the parable Jesus taught. What I do to them, I am doing to Him. What I do not do for them, I am not doing for Him. My God, the conviction on that was strong. When I mistreat my children, I am mistreating Christ, when I yell at my children, I am yelling at Christ. What a hard reality.

God has brought me through and is bringing me through healing for traumas and pain, AND deliverance from ungodly character. He is a great Deliverer!! He is mighty in battle, rich in love and great in POWER! Though God's power is great, when He shows us our issues, pains, and flaws we have to willingly receive the healing. We have to accept deliverance from the darkness in our hearts. He will knock on the door of your heart, but you have to open it. He will hold out His hand to you, but you have to grab it. He will ask you if you want to be made whole, but you have to say yes. Saying yes means that you are willing to change, willing to let go of the pain, willing to repent to people for the ways you have treated them, even if they are "just kids". Receiving healing from God means letting go of the way you have always felt, the ways you have always done things, the way you are…and change.

God brought me face to face with my sin in the way I deal with my children. I said yes to the deliverance He offered me, I repented to him, and my children. I am continuing to seek Him in prayer to help me be a better mother. I am learning to calm my tone, even when the child is wrong. I can give much more clear instruction and impart much more wisdom into my children if I am calm and loving, even when I have to discipline or punish them. I want to be healed from the pain of my childhood, so my children can be raised by an emotionally stable mother. I say yes to my deliverance and yes to being made whole. I am reading and learning more about being a kind and respectful mother.

Your story may be different from mine; your sins may be of a different sort. Whatever your hurts, pains, or shortcomings, the question remains the same. Do you want to be delivered? Do you want to be made whole? Are you willing to take God's hand and walk away from your sin and pains on the path to become a healed woman?

PRAYER

Abba Father, I come to you asking that you would heal me from the hurts and pains that I have suffered in my life and all the ways they affect me. I ask that you would please heal me from all the trauma that riddled my childhood and make me whole. Please forgive me of my sins and the ways I have treated my children, the least of these. I understand that what I do to them I am doing to you. Show me what I lack and give me the fulness of what I need to become the woman and mother you want me to be. In the name of your son Yeshua I pray. Amen.

Be Wise with Money

Looking after your family's money is: planning, spending, and saving every way you can to build wealth and be able to give more

Being wise with money is an area we are growing and maturing in as a family. However, I have always looked for ways to save money for my family. We are not perfect at this, but we try.

Some things we do to save: freezer meals, buying used clothes when we can, DIY as much as possible for haircare, minor home repairs, etc.

Surprise expenses come up, we have all experienced that, and sometimes it feels like there is a faucet that money drains from. There is always something extra to buy or pay for!

This is more reason why it is essential to find ways to save on things you need, find ways to save and put money away.

Every time you save money on something, a big or small amount, that is extra money you can use towards savings or the next thing your family needs.

We all have temptations to overspend, indulge in retail therapy, or just treat ourselves. Using wisdom in spending can help us set examples for our children to follow, teaching them good habits can help them start out on a path to being wise with money as well.

I am not a financial expert by any means, but I do what I can to help conserve. One contribution I make as often as I am able is making freezer meals. I have done once a month cooking, which involves prepping 12–15 dinner meals in freezer bags that I can cook easily in the crock pot when needed. More recently, I focus on cooking our dinner meals for the week. Having meals prepared cuts out reasons to go out to eat which becomes costly and can be very unhealthy long term.

We also gladly accept the free hand me down clothing people offer us as well as shopping at the Salvation Army, mom-to-mom sales, garage sales, Facebook Marketplace, and Craigslist. We still buy new items as well, but we save where we can.

A wise woman saves

A wise woman gives

A wise woman is not focused on consuming, rather conserving

Proverbs 31:20

She stretcheth out her hand to the poor; yea, she reacheth forth her hands to the needy.

Proverbs 21:20

There is treasure to be desired and oil in the dwelling of the wise; but a foolish man spendeth it up.

Proverbs 31

The heart of her husband doth safely trust in her, so that he shall have no need of spoil.

PRAYER

Abba Father, thank you for all the resources you have given us. All that we have comes from you.

Father, please help me to be a wise steward over our family's money. Teach me how to save and show me new ways to conserve our

19

money. As I am saving, help me to continue to give where and when you lead me. God, help me to be a trustworthy woman with money, in the name of your son Yeshua (Jesus), Amen.

Feed Your Family Wisely

*Be mindful of what you feed your family and how
it will affect their health in the future.*

My husband has always done a lot of reading about natural health and healthy eating. I took a nutrition class in college and learned so many new things about eating and health that I never knew before.

Together, we both have tried to do what we know concerning being healthy. We are not always 100% compliant with the wisdom we have, but we have been health conscious overall.

When my second son was around three years old, he started telling us that his stomach hurt quite frequently. He was telling us this so often, we knew we had to do something.

After doing research, we discovered that some people have sensitivity to wheat gluten and that could be the cause of his stomach pains. After careful consideration, we took wheat out of his diet, but it affected all of us.

Subsequently, we realized how much wheat we were eating as a family. We had really been overdoing it! We began to learn more and more about processed wheat, how it can cause inflammation in the body, and many different illnesses and ailments.

Since that time, we have been on a journey to learn about and implement a healthier way of eating. What started with a wheat sensitivity has led to so much more. Over time, I have realized that I am responsible to teach my children what they should and should not eat. Whether they require a special diet or not, their father and I are responsible for teaching them how to eat and live.

One day, it dawned on me that most animals teach their young what to eat and what not to eat. Herbivores, carnivores, and omnivores; they all teach their young in some capacity what is good for them and what is not. They do this without the ability to communicate verbally.

How much more should we as human beings, made in the image of God teach our children how to eat healthy, how to eat to actually feed their bodies, and not just fill their bellies?

This is one of our jobs as parents and it takes a great deal of discipline on our part, because we have to lead by example; but it is so worth it. We have to be mindful of what we feed our family and how it will effect their health in the future.

Please understand, we do not have a perfect diet and we have times of celebration when we eat the fat and drink the sweet (Nehemiah 8:10). But as we live, we are continually just trying to learn and adjust our habits more and more to eat the way God originally intended. The benefits have been immeasurable!

Genesis 1:29

And God said, Behold, I have given you every herb bearing seed, which is upon the face of all the earth, and every tree, in the which is the fruit of a tree yielding seed; to you it shall be for meat.

1 Corinthians 9:27

But I keep under my body, and bring it into subjection: lest that by any means, when I have preached to others, I myself should be a castaway.

Proverbs 25:27

It is not good to eat much honey: so for men to search their own glory is not glory.

3 John 1:2

Beloved, I wish above all things that thou mayest prosper and be in health, even as thy soul prospereth.

1 Corinthians 10:31

Whether therefore ye eat, or drink, or whatsoever ye do, do all to the glory of God.

PRAYER

Abba Father, I thank you for the wisdom in your Word concerning wise eating and health.

Father, you have created the world and all things that are in it, including our bodies. I ask that you would please show us how to have a healthy diet as a family. Give us the will power to resist things that are unhealthy and consume with joy the things that will nourish and strengthen our bodies.

Please help me to lead by example and teach my family healthy habits with the way I eat and live. You are the giver and sustainer of life. We look to you God; all our help comes from you. In the name of your son Yeshua I pray. Amen.

Note: Write down some healthy eating goals that you have for you and your family. Pray over them and ask God to help you achieve them!

The Law of Verbal Kindness

Children need patient and kind parents. This will help them grow up confident and kind with a positive outlook.

Children require a lot of patience. They test every boundary you set. Keeping a level head and being kind at all times can be a tall order to fill. However, through God, all things are possible (Matthew 19:26).

In parenting, one of the most difficult challenges I have faced is overcoming the way I was parented. My parents were amazing and did an amazing job raising me. But they were not perfect, and I have to overcome some of the negative examples they set as I parent my children. The things your parents put in you (good or bad) comes out of you when you have your own children. I tested my parent's patience, now my children are testing mine. How will I respond?

I need to respond with kindness. I am learning that I can be stern when I need to be and still be kind. I don't need to belittle, name call, or degrade my children when I discipline them. I can discipline, train, correct while also encouraging, building them up and speaking life over them. The Bible says that the law of kindness is in the Godly woman's mouth. Not only is she kind with her words, she teaches others how to be kind with their words. I believe God gave women this mandate because we are natural nurturers. But sometimes our flesh gets in the way and we begin to use our mouths as weapons of destruction. So, God gave us a reminder of what our mouths are for in this verse.

PROVERBS 31:26

She openeth her mouth with wisdom; and in her tongue is the law of kindness.

As women of God and as Godly mothers, when we open our mouths, it should be with wisdom and to teach kindness. Wow, I have to simmer in that for a bit.

The question becomes: how do we overcome negative parenting examples we were taught, to become kind, gentle, loving parents? Well, it truly takes the power of God. Some things are so deep rooted that only God's power can break it.

For some of us, negative parenting examples stretch back for generations in our families. If you are willing to grow in this area, and be humble before God, He can heal the wounds that were inflicted upon you as a child and make you whole.

Through prayer, fasting, Godly counsel, reading the word and speaking the word over yourself and your family you can have victory over all forms of abuse you suffered so you do not afflict you children. This is how my deliverance has come.

One objective I have is to parent like I wanted to be parented growing up. Holding to the things my parents did well, while praying to be set free from the things they did not do well.

Another goal I have is to love my children like a grandmother, but train them like a mom.

What does that mean? Well, most grandmothers treat their grandchildren like angels. Being older and wiser, most grandmothers have much more patience than they did raising their own children. So, they speak kindly, they shower the grandchild with love and affirmation, gifts and praise.

This is why most children absolutely love being with grandma and or grandpa. As wonderful as this is, grandmas don't usually do well with guidance, training and discipline. They are too busy having fun with the child. Lol. So that is why I say I want to love my children like a grandma, but train them like a mom. It is just a way to remind myself to be gentle, kind, and affirming, while also giving the guidance, discipline and training they need.

Psalm 68:5–6

A father of the fatherless, and a judge of the widows, is God in his holy habitation.
God setteth the solitary in families: he bringeth out those which are bound with chains: but the rebellious dwell in a dry land

Romans 12:2

And be not conformed to this world: but be ye transformed by the renewing of your mind, that ye may prove what is that good, and acceptable, and perfect, will of God.

Matthew 17:21

Howbeit this kind goeth not out but by prayer and fasting.

Daniel 9:3

And I set my face unto the Lord God, to seek by prayer and supplications, with fasting, and sackcloth, and ashes:

Psalm 147:3–4

He healeth the broken in heart, and bindeth up their wounds.
He telleth the number of the stars; he calleth them all by their names.

Proverbs 15:4

A wholesome tongue is a tree of life: but perverseness therein is a breach in the spirit

PRAYER

Abba Father, I thank you for all that you have brought me through in my life. Thank you for delivering me and helping me. God, I thank you for molding me into the mother you would have me to be.

Thank you, Father, I will receive a kind heart from you, I will receive a kind mouth from you, I receive all that I need to produce Godly seed from the children you have given me.

Father, please bring healing to the wounds in my heart that hinder me from being the mother I want to be. Lord, please heal me, cleanse me, and transform my mind in your word. Help me to love my children with your love and thank you for your love for me. In the name of your son, Yeshua I pray. Amen.

Let Go of Anger Quickly

Do not hold grudges, do not walk in anger.

Children can feel and sense your emotions and how you are feeling toward them. If you get upset, or if the children make you upset, purposefully or by accident, handle the situation quickly.

Pray if you need to, administer discipline, and walk away from it. This allows you and the children to be free to continue to enjoy the day and enjoy each other.

On one occasion, my son did something he was not supposed to, and he knew it. I was very upset with him. I heard in my spirit very clearly to give him a hug. Internally, I was hurt that he would defy me intentionally.

Looking into his beautiful face, I remembered how excited I was when he was born, I thought he was one of the most amazing things I had ever seen with my eyes. Now, here I was nine years later, seething with anger towards him. Again, the voice spoke, give him a hug.

Despite my anger, I obeyed. As soon as we embraced, the shell of anger cracked, and the fragments were blown away. This was my son that I gave birth to, and I love him even when he makes mistakes.

Ephesians 4:26 Be angry, and sin not: let not the sun go down upon your wrath:

28

Over time, I have been growing in releasing myself to continue the day in joy, and inviting the children to continue the day in joy after discipline or punishments. It has been a blessing for all of us, and an opportunity for personal growth for me as well.

There were many days when I spent the entire day upset after one of my children was disobedient. Especially if there were multiple problems with the same child. However, I have come to realize that if I allow myself to continue this way, I will literally spend all my days angry. What a thief of the precious time I have with my children!

I don't want to regret missing opportunities to bond and create memories with my children because I gave anger all my energy. God is too good for that.

Psalm 30:4–5

Sing unto the Lord, O ye saints of his, and give thanks at the remembrance of his holiness.
   For his anger endureth but a moment; in his favour is life: weeping may endure for a night, but joy cometh in the morning.

Matthew 5:22

But I say unto you, That whosoever is angry with his brother without a cause shall be in danger of the judgment: and whosoever shall say to his brother, Raca, shall be in danger of the council: but whosoever shall say, Thou fool, shall be in danger of hell fire.

PRAYER

Abba Father, I thank you that your mercy for me is new today. Thank you that your anger endures but for a moment. I rejoice that I can come to you repenting and find forgiveness and favor.

Father, I thank you for helping me to be like you, to be slow to anger, rich in mercy, and quick to forgive. Let me not be angry with my children without cause and have mercy upon them as I consider their frame and that they are growing and learning. Help our home to be filled with singing and rejoicing in your holiness. Let me not go to bed angry at anyone, especially my own family. In the name of your son, Yeshua I pray. Amen.

10

Don't Be Afraid to Grow

*As we grow and progress in life, we are usually
excited about maturing to different levels.*

When we go from grade school to junior high, junior high to high school, and high school to college, we all look forward to each new step. We usually never try to revert backwards.

Motherhood should be seen as a new level in life, a new step as we matriculate through life. We should not spend one day trying to go back. We should not resent our children, wishing we were still single, or childless. If you don't mature, you stagnate.

The married woman with children should not feel like her life is less fulfilling than a single woman's career. You are in a different phase. Please receive the maturation that this phase offers and be glad about progress.

As a mother, I have had to make many decisions about my life, the direction of my family and my role in all of it. Many things I thought were important to me, I had to let go.

Many of the dreams that I thought were my right to achieve have died and been buried.

Many things I thought were vital components of my personality, were simply vanity masquerading as qualities.

God has transformed me, my life, and everything I held dear.

I graduated from college one month before my wedding. My husband was an entrepreneur and I had aspirations of starting a clothing line. We were both driven, determined and supportive of each other's goals.

After having my first child, I started reading and praying for an anointing for motherhood. Being a mother was much harder than I expected, and it was clear to me that I was unprepared for the sacrifice and death to self that motherhood required.

When I had my second child, the Lord began showing me the consequences if I continued focusing the desires of my heart on success in fashion. He showed me that a lot of what I was reaching for was because I wanted to feel successful in front of those who knew me.

With the guidance of the Holy Spirit, I realized that in order to bear the Godly fruit that God wants (Malachi 2:15), I needed to devote my attention to my husband, children, and home; in that order.

This felt hard for me at the time. It was hard for me to let things die that I wanted for so long, it was hard for me to lay down my desires, and to solely focus on the little ones He had given us.

Looking back on it, I now realize that stepping fully into motherhood, without holding onto anything else to make me feel accomplished was a huge stepping-stone to becoming the woman God has called me to be, instead of the woman I wanted to be. There is a huge difference.

God had to undo all the lies in my soul about what a woman was supposed to be, who I was, and what God expected of me versus the messages I had gotten my entire life about womanhood from American society.

You can have it all. Right? Wrong. Not at the same time.

The truth is that you are one person, and sometimes when we try and give everything our all. Something will suffer, and sometimes it's the children that suffer when we are splitting our time between raising them and chasing dreams.

Everyone has different circumstances in their life. Some women must work, some choose to work, and some just like to be busy and have lots of things to do.

Sit in prayer and ask God, "Are the choices I am making strengthening or hindering my investment into my children?"

Ask God what He wants from you. How does He want your family to be structured?

Does God want you to work or stay home? What does your husband want?

Ask Him and receive His answer with a humble heart. It may take lots of time in prayer, and maybe fasting, but pray until He answers. He may speak through your husband.

Motherhood is not a demotion or a low-class profession that women apply for when they don't have skills or education.

Motherhood is a calling, a powerful force in the earth to help raise, disciple, educate and equip the next generation of world changers for the kingdom of God. Be honored that God has called you forth for this time, to raise His warriors.

Ecclesiastes 11:9–10

Rejoice, O young man, in thy youth; and let thy heart cheer thee in the days of thy youth, and walk in the ways of thine heart, and in the sight of thine eyes: but know thou, that for all these things God will bring thee into judgment.

Therefore remove sorrow from thy heart, and put away evil from thy flesh: for childhood and youth are vanity.

Psalm 127

Except the Lord build the house, they labour in vain that build it: except the Lord keep the city, the watchman waketh but in vain.

It is vain for you to rise up early, to sit up late, to eat the bread of sorrows: for so he giveth his beloved sleep.

Lo, children are an heritage of the Lord: and the fruit of the womb is his reward.

As arrows are in the hand of a mighty man; so are children of the youth.

Happy is the man that hath his quiver full of them: they shall not be ashamed, but they shall speak with the enemies in the gate.

Psalm 113:9

He maketh the barren woman to keep house, and to be a joyful mother of children. Praise ye the Lord.

PRAYER

Abba Father, thank you for everything you are teaching me. Thank you for your leading and guidance. You have all power of heaven and earth in your hands. Yahuah, I humble myself to you and I ask, am I positioned the way you want me to be in my home? Is my work pleasing in your sight? What would you have me to change, Lord?

You are God alone. Please remove all blindness from my eyes and unstop my ears that I may hear what your Spirit is saying to me. Cleanse me from the lies of feminism, false doctrine, and bad examples. Let me not follow my own ways but follow the path you have set for me. Show me your desires for my work in my family and give me the strength and fear of the Lord to obey you. In the name of your son Yashua I pray. Amen.

Following Emotions can Lead to Perversion

*Putting your child's feelings or emotions above
obedience to the Lord is vile before God.*

Honoring your children's immature emotional desires above teaching them obedience and Godly character is a welcome mat for sin and iniquity to continue and proliferate in the next generation.

Read the full story of Eli and his wicked sons: 1 Samuel 2–4

1 Samuel 3:13

For I have told him that I will judge his house for ever for the iniquity which he knoweth; because his sons made themselves vile, and he restrained them not.

Proverbs 29:15

The rod and reproof give wisdom: but a child left to himself bringeth his mother to shame.

Our culture is obsessed with youth, the wonder of childhood, and teaching fables and lies to children on the guise of stimulating their imagination. However, children have spirits and need to be taught to follow God, His Word, and Commandments.

Their souls need to be made alive in Christ, not the wicked imaginations of man. Children have the ability to understand the truth if you teach them. Children have the ability to walk in the truth if you are a faithful guide and lead them. Children have the ability to become students of the word of God, if you feed them.

God has been leading us and transforming our lives as a family. Two of the major things He did was lead us to completely stop celebrating Christmas (we already forsook Easter and Halloween), not because we don't love celebrations, but because of the link to idolatry.

Another thing we were instructed to do in the Bible was to get rid of graven images (statues, figurines, stuffed animals, pendants, wall hangings, etc.). God forbade the making, keeping or worship of anything in the shape of an animal, human, fish, or bird, or other creature (Exodus 20:4, Romans 1:23).

God has been helping us to grow as parents in leading our children, instead of being led by our children.

If we had hearts to please our children above pleasing God, we would not have been able to obey God on these issues, or many other things He has led us to do as parents.

Teaching your children to follow God and not their feelings is essential. It is one of the most basic lessons on being a true disciple of Christ.

My mother got saved when I was around five years old. Soon after she became saved, she learned the idolatrous roots of Christmas, Easter, and Halloween. She decided then that we were done. She told us that we would no longer be celebrating these holidays and let us celebrate each holiday one last time and we were done.

Did it ruin my childhood? No. It actually was a building block towards a set apart life. We are not called to blend with the world as much as possible. We are called to come out, be separate, and shine light in the world (2 Corinthians 6:17; Philippians 2:15).

It does feel difficult to lead your child down a different path than most of their peers, friends, and cousins are on. But if you want different results, you must do something different.

When a Godly man and woman get married, God is looking for Godly seed to come from that union.

You cannot raise your children according to the standards of the world and expect truly Godly fruit. You cannot regard how your child may feel about something higher than you regard God's Living Word.

As we saw with Eli, the consequences can be dire. If you do not teach your children to follow Christ and obey the commandments of Yahuah, they will follow the culture instead, and eventually cast Jesus to the side.

> *Psalm 119:9*
>
> *⁹ Wherewithal shall a young man cleanse his way? by taking heed thereto according to thy word.*
>
> *Psalm 119:105*
>
> *¹⁰⁵ Thy word is a lamp unto my feet, and a light unto my path.*

PRAYER

Abba Father, I praise you because your word is alive and able to light our path. Thank you for teaching us your ways God! Lord, please help me to lead my children based on your word, not my own thoughts or their feelings.

God, bless me to be strong and courageous as I train up my children in the way they should go. Please do not let my child's changing attitudes and emotions effect my decision making but let your unwavering word in action in our lives change us. In the name of your son Yeshua I pray. Amen.

Overcoming Generational Abuse

*Use God's Mercy and Grace to break the
negative cycles in your bloodline.*

This is a sensitive topic that affects many, so I touch on this with great sensitivity and care. Many children are abused in different ways growing up, sometimes without realizing it until they are older. The abuse we suffer can follow us into our own parenting journey if we allow it to. It is very important that you are aware of the patterns of abuse from your childhood so you can be healed and not repeat the same mistakes with your children.

My mother and her siblings suffered heavy physical abuse under my grandmother when they were growing up. My mother, aunts, and uncles all told stories of how badly my grandmother would talk to them and beat them. They were all so wounded; some got it worse than others. But they all suffered a lot as children.

My mother was aware of her abuse, and intentionally tried to do better and she did. However, she did not overcome her abuse completely. She was still verbally and physically abusive towards us to a degree. Yelling, degrading, name calling, and spankings that went too far and lasted too long. She did not do all the things her mother did, but she did not get fully delivered either.

I remember feeling devalued as a child. On one hand, my mother showed me great love most of the time. But when she flared up and was verbally or physically abusive, I felt like I could not fully trust her and hardness built up in my heart.

In college, God began to touch my heart and bring to the surface some of the issues I had from my childhood and upbringing. To this day, I am still fighting and praying for full deliverance myself. Generational abuse is not unique to my family. Many parents abuse because they were abused, and their parents were abused. We have to stop and look at what is happening, each generation being broken, hurt, and given pain that they will have to fight through for the rest of their lives. When will the cycle end?

Well, it can end with you.

One step to ending the cycle is first acknowledging the fact that you were abused. Verbal abuse, mental abuse, physical abuse, and sexual abuse. Acknowledge these things to God in prayer, journal, and write it down if that helps. What painful memories do you have from your childhood? Were these moments of abuse? How did it effect you, change you, and make you feel? Take these things to God in prayer, also. Then, begin to ask Yah for healing for those wounds in your heart. Ask Him to show you how these things affect you as a parent. Ask Him to deliver you from all evil that has built up in your heart, and teach you how to resist the devil, so you do not also walk in a spirit of abuse and damage the next generation.

When you have your own children, the way you were raised tries to surface, rather good or bad. I know that is the case for me. The good and bad things my parents did all try to surface, and sometimes you feel like you are turning into your parents. But as a mature adult, it is important to realize that you are in control of your emotions. You cannot blame your children for your responses. You should be in control of your mouth and body at all times; period. Realizing this has been a huge step in helping me overcome generational abuse. Not giving myself a license to yell, scream, or go off the handle.

Excuses like "They made me mad", "They pushed my buttons", "They made me flip out" are exactly that; EXCUSES. Self-control is a fruit of the Holy Spirit. So even when our children act up or do things they are not supposed to do, we should still be in control of how we respond and administer appropriate discipline in love, and under control. A lack of self-control is your issue, not your child's.

Something else that has helped me is remembering how I felt as a child when I was yelled at, put down, or abused. I don't want my children feeling the pain I felt. With the power of God, I must be made whole so I can change the course of my family and be free to stop the generational curse of child abuse.

If you are married, talking to your husband about your past and how it is affects you as a mother is important. You can ask him to pray for you and give you accountability as you grow and break free from the cycle of abuse. Talk to him about how you want to handle discipline, make a plan together, and hold one another accountable to the Godly standards you set. Your husband may be in the same place, needing to overcome generational abuse. If that is the case, pray through these things together, submit to God together, be healed and delivered together, and seek to raise up healthy, whole children together.

If you are not married, please reach out to a Godly woman or friend who you trust to talk to about these issues. Someone who can pray for you and hold you accountable to the plan of action you set to change.

For some women, therapy or counseling may be a needed step in overcoming child abuse. Counseling can really help in getting to the root of certain problems in your life and helping you find a way to move forward. If you feel that would be helpful for you, I encourage you to seek out a Christian counselor with great references who can help you and give you Godly counsel.

You have the power through Christ to overcome any abuse you may have suffered.

James 4:6–10

⁶ But he giveth more grace. Wherefore he saith,
    God resisteth the proud, but giveth grace
    unto the humble.
⁷ Submit yourselves therefore to God. Resist the
    devil, and he will flee from you.

⁸ Draw nigh to God, and he will draw nigh to you. Cleanse your hands, ye sinners; and purify your hearts, ye double minded.

⁹ Be afflicted, and mourn, and weep: let your laughter be turned to mourning, and your joy to heaviness.

¹⁰ Humble yourselves in the sight of the Lord, and he shall lift you up

STEPS TO TAKE FROM JAMES 4

- Submit your issues to God
- Stop listening to the devil, the demons of abuse, the example of abuse that may have been set for you.
- When you stop listening to the devil, he must flee!
- Grow closer to God through prayer, fasting and reading the Bible, and He will draw close to you!
- It is good to feel sad and convicted for the wrong things you may have done to your children, that shows the work of God's conviction in your life.
- Be humble before God, cry out to Him for His help and guidance, and He will lift you from your situation!

It is important to consistently bring these things to Yahuah whenever they surface in your life to attain full deliverance and healing. This shows you are always growing and receiving His help and leadership so your family can be the best it can possibly be and you can be the Godly mother He is calling you to be!

PRAYER

Abba Father, I thank you that I can come to you for help. Thank you that you are a faithful Father who will never leave me. Yah, I submit all negative experiences and any abuse I suffered to you as a child. My parents hurt me in many ways God, and I need healing from you. I need to be delivered from a hard heart. Please replace it with a soft heart that can receive guidance from you on this issue. God, I want to be made whole and break the cycle of abuse.

Please forgive me for any way that I may have abused my children, knowingly or unknowingly. Please deliver me and help me to resist to urge to yell, name call, or physically abuse my children, even when they misbehave. I humble myself to you, Father, please lift me out of the curse of child abuse and make me whole. In the name of your Son, Yeshua I pray. Amen.

Sow Good Seeds Into Your Children

The good seeds you sow today…
Will be the flowers they bring you tomorrow.

Love, joy, peace, long suffering, gentleness, goodness, faith, meekness, and self-control ladies! Those are the seeds we want to sow daily!

How do we sow good seeds in our children?

The seeds we sow are teaching them the word of God, living the word of God in front of them, and in interactions with them. There are so many ways to sow good seeds of the Word into your children:

- Speak to your children with kindness, even when they make mistakes or disobey.
- Speak God's word over your children.
- Treat others with kindness, knowing that they are learning from your example.
- If you are married, honor and respect your husband.
- Reading the Word of God to them daily.
- Teach them to pray and worship.
- Teach them to speak and live the word of God.

- As you sow good seeds, and as you surround them with a Godly community that are also sowing good seeds into them, you must wait for God to give the increase to it.

Just like with natural seeds, people plant them and water them and God makes them grow. It is the same with sewing the word of God into your children, or any soul for that matter.

Conversely, the bad seeds you sow will also bring forth fruit, although there will be no rejoicing when that fruit is harvested.

Negative comments, complaining, rebellious words and actions, emotional, physical, or mental abuse, impatience. Our children are watching and observing all that we do. They are being affected by our attitudes daily even if they do not show it right away. In time though, the fruit of our negative thoughts, words and actions will show in our children in some way.

My oldest son once told me that when I am upset, he feels like he is affected in the spirit realm. This is a very deep statement for a then nine-year-old to make.

I was surprised at his articulation of what he felt, but I was not at all surprised by the statement. I can feel when I get upset and start grumbling, fussing, and complaining and how it shifts the atmosphere in my house.

Our husbands and children are greatly affected by our attitudes, emotions, and actions. This is why the Bible says it is better to be on the rooftop than in the house with a brawling woman (Proverbs 21:9).

Once we realize that the position of influence, we have in our home is powerful enough to change the lives of those around us, we can seize the privilege of bearing precious seed that will bring forth good fruit for God.

We can have peace as we cook and clean, knowing that our daughters are watching and being trained on how to have a good attitude when it is time for them to work in their homes someday.

We can speak to our sons with respect, even when we discipline them, knowing that how we communicate with them is training them on what treatment to tolerate from their future wives, as well as how they will treat all women.

We will have joy as we minister to our husbands, knowing that the love, respect, and honor we show them helps to build them and strengthen them as the glory and covering of our children.

Be prayerful as you plant good seeds in your family, so you can reap a great reward as you watch your children mature in Christ and become Godly men and women that treat people with respect and show the love of God.

The good seeds you sow today
Will be the flowers they bring you tomorrow.
The bad seeds you sow will sprout up
And bring you sorrow.
Sow good seeds in your children
And you can rejoice in years to come.

Galatians 6:6–9

Be not deceived; God is not mocked: for whatsoever a man soweth, that shall he also reap.

For he that soweth to his flesh shall of the flesh reap corruption; but he that soweth to the Spirit shall of the Spirit reap life everlasting.

And let us not be weary in well doing: for in due season we shall reap, if we faint not.

PRAYER

Abba Father, I praise you, you are a good Father and a good shepherd. Father, thank you for teaching me to apply your word to my life. God, please anoint me to plant good seeds into my children. Please help me to water the good seeds that are there.

I praise you in advance for the great harvest I will reap in my children, and I thank you for letting me not be weary in well doing. Help me to walk in the Spirit and show the fruits of the Spirit in all that I do in my home, In the name of your son, Yeshua I pray. Amen.

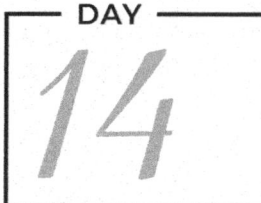
Lay Down Your Life

No Greater Love has a man than this, that he
would lay down his life for his friends.

Motherhood requires a laying down of a woman's life. Motherhood is such a great **opportunity.**

Motherhood is an opportunity to learn how to put others before yourself.

1 Thessalonians 5:14

Now we exhort you, brethren, warn them that
are unruly, comfort the feebleminded, support
the weak, be patient toward all men.

Motherhood is an opportunity to learn how to build, strengthen and encourage others.

Motherhood is an opportunity to learn how to walk in love at all times.

Ephesians 5:2

And walk in love, as Christ also hath loved us,
and hath given himself for us an offering and
a sacrifice to God for a sweetsmelling savour.

The question then becomes, can we humble ourselves enough to recognize and take advantage of these opportunities?

In the moment when we are stressed, tired, have a million and one things on our plate and the toddler spills milk all over the floor, can we respond in love?

Can we look past our suffering and minister to them with kindness on our tongues? Seeing their need for love and affirmation is more important than our need to get things done.

Can we trust that as we care for them, God will take care of ALL things that concern us?

I have failed this many times, to see the opportunity for personal growth in serving my children. I have failed at times in putting their needs before my own. However, I believe that recognizing my failure is the first step to victory.

When you recognize where you have failed, you can then turn and sin no more. But if you don't know you are going the wrong way, you will never turn around.

John 15:13

No Greater Love has a man than this, that he would lay down his life for his friends.

PRAYER

Abba Father, I pray that I will recognize and take advantage of the opportunities to show love, to serve, and to be kind under pressure that motherhood presents.

Also, that I would sit at your feet and place relationship with you and loving people over the things I want to get done. Thank you, Lord, I trust that as I seek you first, as I put the needs of others before myself, that you will care for me and meet all my needs. In the name of your son Yeshua I pray. Amen.

Choose Joy Every Day

Choose joy. Joy is a choice.

Romans 15:13

Now the God of hope fill you with all joy and peace in believing, that ye may abound in hope, through the power of the Holy Ghost.

Philippians 4:4

Rejoice in the Lord always: and again I say, Rejoice.

Joyfulness has never come naturally for me. I have always been a very serious, contemplative, and moody person. As a small baby and toddler, I always had a very serious and stern look on my face. So much so that people would ask my father what was wrong with me. I laugh about that now; that has always been me.

Don't get me wrong, I love to laugh and have fun with people, but in general I am a very serious person. The prophetic gifting I have comes into play in the presentation of seriousness in my personality. My children are also heavily gifted in the prophetic. As you can imagine, a house full of moody prophets can be a bit of a challenge.

I see now more than ever that joy is a necessary ingredient in the life of a believer.

Joy enables us to appreciate the beautiful things God has done, the beauty and life in His creation. Joy gives us emotional and mental strength to get through life's challenges. Joy is a byproduct of being in the presence of the Most High.

What do you do when joy does not come naturally to you? You choose to take it anyway! I have been practicing having joy, and it makes all the difference. Smiling when you don't feel like it, speaking positive things when you really want to comment on the negative, and choosing to see the good qualities in those around you. Thanking God throughout the day for the things you recognize His hand on.

All these things can help you practice joy, until it becomes a natural part of your life. It does feel fake at first but press on, you and your family need it. It is kind of like putting food on your plate at a buffet. You can pick what you put on your plate and what you eat. Can you choose what attitude you walk in daily and what you are going to feast on?

Will you choose to feast on the things that are lovely and of good report, or the things that are getting on your nerves?

Walking in joy is so important because it will also will help strengthen those around you and make them feel good in your presence (Psalm 33:1).

God has been helping me to realize that I want to be the kind of mother that my children want to be around when they are adults. I want them to feel blessed, loved, and encouraged in my presence. I don't want them dreading the thought of coming to visit me because I am negative and drag them down emotionally. We have to build in the beginning with the end in mind.

Ask yourself: how can you improve in choosing joy?

PRAYER

Abba Father, I thank you for your word, thank you for transforming me with it. God you are good and worthy of all praise. I pray today that you would teach me and my family how to choose to be joyful. I want the strength that joy brings, and the beauty of praise in holiness to be in our home. Let singing, rejoicing, and laughter fill our hearts and our days. In the name of your son, Yeshua I pray. Amen.

Everyone Needs Love Every Day

We all want to be loved, accepted, celebrated, and embraced.

On those difficult days when your child's behavior pushes you to the brink of frustration, remember they need love, acceptance, embrace, and celebration!

Give them the discipline they need when they misbehave, then push past it and continue giving them what they need: love and understanding.

Children are under a lot of stress and pressure to obey and perform up to standard without full understanding of how everything works. Teaching and training them sometimes takes top priority, but children also need to be understood.

Understanding their heart and where their thoughts were at in a particular situation can help them trust that you have their best interest at heart. If we as moms approach each encounter with our children with a desire to love them and help them grow, then our discipline will be based on what is best for them.

Children often misbehave, but it is not always on purpose. Sometimes they did not fully understand the instructions you gave them. Maybe there was a legitimate reason they seemingly disobeyed or perhaps they truly did forget. Whatever the case is, if you are patient, calm, and discerning, you can help your child grow in situations of discipline and with Godly discernment. Then you can give a fair punishment if one is needed.

Just as quick as we administer punishments when a child does something wrong, be even more diligent to celebrate and congratulate them when they do what's right. When they share, when they show love, and when they are polite, shower them with praise.

This will help them continue to develop in confidence in times of frequent correction. It will also reassure them of your love and, acceptance, and respect for them.

> *Ephesians 4:32*
>
> *And be ye kind one to another, tenderhearted, forgiving one another, even as God for Christ's sake hath forgiven you.*
>
> *Micah 6:8*
>
> *He hath shewed thee, O man, what is good; and what doth the Lord require of thee, but to do justly, and to love mercy, and to walk humbly with thy God?*

PRAYER

Abba Father, I praise you because you delight in mercy. You forgive me when I repent, and you love me with an everlasting love. Thank you, Heavenly Father, that I will be just in my home, love mercy and walk in humility with my children. You are so gracious and kind, help me to be like you Father. In the name of your son, Yeshua I pray. Amen.

Healing from Loss

You can have joy after your sorrow.

Losing a pregnancy, a full-term baby, a newborn, toddler, or child are devastating events that have brought deep grief and sadness to many mothers. Loss is sometimes a surprising twist on the journey of motherhood. If you have never experienced loss, I rejoice with you! But if you have, you are not alone.

My story is not unique as many women have lost multiple pregnancies. There is courage in community and in our testimonies of how God brought us out. So, I share this for the moms who have faced loss, as a way of weeping with you. I share it for women who have walked with friends or family members through their loss. God is our light in the darkest of nights, and in Him we have healing, restoration and one day, joy.

My first loss was Love Anna. I carried her for 24 weeks. Around 20 weeks, I found out that she had a genetic abnormality that would make it almost impossible for her to make it full term. The doctor told me if by chance she was born alive, she would die soon after birth. I did not want to accept or believe what he said. I cried uncontrollably, but somehow, I thought she would prove the doctor wrong and overcome. My husband and I prayed and cried out to God. We set our faith that she would live. We lost her on July 25, 2019.

In December 2019, I became pregnant again. My family and I were overjoyed. The pregnancy was going perfect. I had light spotting but the doctors were convinced there was nothing wrong with baby. At my 20-week anatomy scan I was told there was no heartbeat. It felt unreal to hear that same phrase in an ultrasound again.

Numbness, pain, distress, anger. There was nowhere I could hide; pain was all around me.

My testimony is not that my babies miraculously came back to life, although God is capable of that. My testimony is that God walked me through the darkest of nights and brought me out with my hands raised in worship, from days when I literally thought I would never smile or laugh again.

He brought me out, he brought our family out. And I tell you, He can bring you out.

Cry out, pray, scream, ask Him to help, you, heal you, comfort you. He rescued me, and He can rescue you too, Sis.

If you believe in Him, call out to Him, ask for forgiveness and deliverance, He will be your help in trouble. Even if your loss was years ago, and you've had other babies since then, there may still be healing you need in your heart. God is able to reach you.

Yah gave me a very comforting dream while our family was going through this difficult time.

I dreamed I was in deep water with my husband. Everything was pitch black and he was leading me through the deep. We came to a rock wall that extended out of the sea. I climbed up onto the rock wall and stood up. I began to walk.

It was so dark I could not see where my feet were landing. With each step I did not know if my foot would land on solid rock or ocean waters. But every step I took, there was solid rock under my feet. My husband watched from the water, amazed, and encouraging me to keep walking.

A while after I had the dream, I was talking with a friend of mine that was giving me encouragement. She mentioned Psalm 77 during our conversation. It blew me away when I realized that the Scripture lined up with what Yah showed me in my dream.

I want to encourage you that when you face loss, and you are suffering through a storm or storms of grief, you can cry out to God and He will hear you. After losing my mom and two babies, many nights I cried and I could not sleep. I felt like I would sink into a pit of sorrow, and not be able to escape unless God rescued me.

Every time, EVERYTIME I called, He answered, always in a fresh way that revived me.

Psalm 77

¹ I cried unto God with my voice, even unto God with my voice; and he gave ear unto me.

² In the day of my trouble I sought the Lord: my sore ran in the night, and ceased not: my soul refused to be comforted.

³ I remembered God, and was troubled: I complained, and my spirit was overwhelmed. Selah.

⁴ Thou holdest mine eyes waking: I am so troubled that I cannot speak.

⁵ I have considered the days of old, the years of ancient times.

⁶ I call to remembrance my song in the night: I commune with mine own heart: and my spirit made diligent search.

⁷ Will the Lord cast off for ever? and will he be favourable no more?

⁸ Is his mercy clean gone for ever? doth his promise fail for evermore?

⁹ Hath God forgotten to be gracious? hath he in anger shut up his tender mercies? Selah.

¹⁰ And I said, This is my infirmity: but I will remember the years of the right hand of the most High.

¹¹ I will remember the works of the Lord: surely I will remember thy wonders of old.

¹² I will meditate also of all thy work, and talk of thy doings.

¹³ Thy way, O God, is in the sanctuary: who is so great a God as our God?
¹⁴ Thou art the God that doest wonders: thou hast declared thy strength among the people.
¹⁵ Thou hast with thine arm redeemed thy people, the sons of Jacob and Joseph. Selah.
¹⁶ The waters saw thee, O God, the waters saw thee; they were afraid: the depths also were troubled.
¹⁷ The clouds poured out water: the skies sent out a sound: thine arrows also went abroad.
18 The voice of thy thunder was in the heaven: the lightnings lightened the world: the earth trembled and shook.
¹⁹ Thy way is in the sea, and thy path in the great waters, and thy footsteps are not known.
²⁰ Thou leddest thy people like a flock by the hand of Moses and Aaron.

If you have suffered infant loss pray this with me. If not, pray for a friend or family member who has.

PRAYER

Abba Father, the loss of my baby is heavy and painful. God, I cannot be healed on my own, I cannot carry this burden of grief on my own. I ask that you would please forgive me of all my sins, and heal my broken heart.

Father, you are my hope and I look to you, because all of my help comes from you and only you can touch this pain. In the name of your son, Yeshua I pray. Amen.

This is a Dream Job!

Treat motherhood like your dream job, invest all of your gifts, talents and resources into it.

Titus 2:5

To be discreet, chaste, <u>keepers at home</u>, good, obedient to their own husbands, that the word of God be not blasphemed

Proverbs 31:27a

She looketh well to the ways of her household…

Before I had children, I had dreams of being a fashion designer. I worked as a fashion stylist for a side job and I always loved home decorating. After having my first two children, I continued to pursue fashion, and even hosted and produced a television show about fashion through a local television station.

My husband always supported and encouraged me. He helped to push me and wanted me to grow and produce with all the gifts God has given me. As busy as I was using my talents in industry, God began to make it abundantly clear that it was time to focus on my family and trade my dreams for His.

Producing a television show was fun for me. Although I was producing my television show on a local television station, I was still excited about the show's potential. However, planning the shows and doing all the production work besides taping was beginning to take up more and more time and was becoming difficult to manage with an infant and toddler to care for.

Not wanting to give up, I was determined to make it work and push. I was determined to use the degree in fashion I had worked for and was in debt for. I was just beginning to fine tune and improve my shows overall quality.

At that point, God told me to stop. God gave me a dream:

> *I was dressed up, some friends from college were on a balcony above me. I was spinning and twirling to get their attention. While I was twirling for my audience, I failed to see a huge hole in the ground. My youngest son was crawling towards the hole and I did not notice. He fell in, and by the time I saw it, it was too late, I could not get him out.*

What was God saying to me? What was He showing me in that dream? He was showing me that I was focused on myself when I needed to be focused on my home and children.

Getting the attention of others so they could view me as successful was putting my family at risk. I didn't know if it was a natural threat or a spiritual threat, but God made it clear that my children—specifically my second son—was being put at risk as I pursued my dreams.

Also, around this time a very well known, Emmy-award winning news anchor hired me to be her stylist. One night, I was at her home going through her wardrobe. I took a little break and she and I were talking. I was pregnant with my second child at the time, and we were talking about children and family. She mentioned to me that she wished she had stopped working when her daughter was born. I looked at her with bewilderment and asked why. At that time, I was still in my fashion mogul mindset and really looked up to this woman; she had a career most can only dream of.

She said, "Yes, I wish I had stopped working when I had my daughter. My husband has a great job and could have supported us. I did not have to work. Now my daughter is a senior in high school and about to go to college and I have lost all that time with her and I can't get it back". This shook my heart. I went home in awe, thinking about what she had said. This was one of the turning points in my mindset. If this woman regretted losing time with her child, despite her tremendous success, I didn't want to have those same regrets. This along with the dream I shared helped me make the decision to plant my heart in my home and invest my life into building my family instead of a business, brand, or career. We think we can have it all, but we cannot.

When my second son was around seven months old, I stopped production on my show, stopped working as a stylist, stopped pursuing building a clothing line, and obeyed the leading of the Lord.

That was eight years ago. Over this time, I have learned that my home is a worthy place for me to use my gifts and all the talents the Lord has given me.

Once my heart was settled in my home and I was content being a keeper at home, I was able to see all the ways I could use my passions to build my family and create a beautiful home for us to live in.

I share this testimony with you as an invitation to use what God has given you to build the family God has given you with the same passion you would if you were the CEO of a top company in your field of interest. Treat motherhood like your dream job, invest all your gifts, talents, and resources into it.

I'm not saying it's a sin for a woman to work. But work should be due to necessity. If your husband needs help to pay bills, if he is laid off and can't find work, or if you are single and must take care of things on your own, do what you need to do.

The work I was doing was not necessary, but rather by choice. I wanted to use my degree, I wanted to promote a business, and I wanted to feel like I was doing something that mattered. When in reality not one of those things was as important and caring for my children and being present to support my husband.

Having talked to many women over the years, it is clear that a lot of women work, not because they have to, but because they want to. There is a big difference. Many women use work as a way to escape from the pressures of home life. More than one woman has told me to my face that staying home is too hard and they work to get away from their children. Escaping, not cherishing, and rejecting home life instead of being a keeper of it. Valuing career over family this is the heart issue that needs to be addressed.

What is your Why?

- Do you work to feel important? You are far more import-ant to your children than your boss or customers. You are the only mother they have. You are totally replaceable at your job.
- Do you work because you paid for an expensive degree? The cost of your children feeling neglected, the cost of your children lacking support they need from you, the cost of wasted years, and lost time you can never recover with them is far greater.
- Do you work because you fought so hard to get where you are, and you cannot tolerate the thought of losing what you've worked for? Your child needs you to put that energy and focus into building them up, building your family so you can reap great rewards that are deeper than a bonus at work.

Rea life encounters with women:

I went to the doctor for a check-up. I was chatting with my doctor who was a young mother with two babies. She was telling me that she had a hard time getting to work that morning because her daughter cries so much when she gets dropped off at day care. The doctor told me she was married and her husband works also. I asked her why doesn't she stay home with her children? Especially since it seems that her daughter needs her. She replied, "I can't, I have done too much for my career, and I can't give it up".

This conversation broke my heart. It really showed the displaced priorities we have as women. This mother loves her children, very much, I do not doubt that. But this subtle ideology has crept into her heart, career first, family on the side. We really have to evaluate why we are doing what we are doing. If you are your family's only means of support, you have to do what you need to. I know many single mothers cry, wishing they could stay home with their babies, and my heart goes out to those mamas. Those who can stay home and raise their children, should be more appreciative for the opportunity! Raising a family is an opportunity to impact generations.

Once, when I was out shopping at a large store, I asked a worker for help. The woman came over and helped me find what I was looking for. She was very nice and we began to talk. She told me about herself and that she only worked to get out of the house and away from her children. She had quite a few children; this shocked me. She seemed so nice and mature, but her statements revealed a lot. Now, I know better than anyone, that getting a break can help recharge you, refresh you, and make you better for your family! I make a habit of getting out by myself on a regular basis. This is important, burnout is real.

However, there is a difference between getting out to rest and recharge and running away. One mindset says, this job is so important I want to give my best, so I need to go recharge and rest. The other mindset says, this is too hard and I can't wait to get away from this house! The first mindset honors the position of home builder, the other makes light of it and rejects it. Do you see the difference? God is all knowing, and He searches what's in our hearts.

Encouragement for single mothers:

If you have to work because you are on your own, but you want to be there for your children as much as possible, begin to pray and ask God how you can accomplish this. God can give you a strategy! Perhaps you can find a job that has school time hours, and you can get off in time to be with your children after school. Or perhaps you can start a home-based business or daycare which would allow you to work and still spend as much time as possible with your babies. If you have a heart to build your home, I believe Yahuah can give you the blueprints!

Whether you are a trained accountant, teacher, principle, lawyer, doctor, or fashion designer, God can show you ways to use what you have to build His dream, your family. Your gifts and degree do not have to go to waste! Your family is your new business, do this work with all your might!

PRAYER

Abba Father, I thank you so much for all the gifts and talents you have given me. I am the work of your hands, and I am fearfully and wonderfully made. Lord, I submit all that I am to you. I submit my career, dreams, and goals to you.

I ask that you would lead and guide me in what you would have me to do. How you would have me use my gifts to honor you and serve my family. Lord, I want to be a virtuous woman that looks well to the ways of her household. In the name of your son, Yeshua I pray. Amen.

Giving Your Motherhood Sacrifice in Faith

A willing sacrifice...the sacrifice has to be with a willing heart.
Your faith is what enables you to have joy in your sacrifice.

Faith moves you forward when you feel like giving up. Faith helps you take one more step when you feel like you cannot do anymore. Faith keeps you looking up and filled with hope when you see that spark of possibility underneath a pile of doubts. When you have faith, and believe in what you are doing, it makes the sacrifices you make easier to bear.

The willingness of the sacrifice comes from the heart. If the sacrifice is with reluctance, frustration, fear and anger, then depression and regret will set in.

But if you say in your heart, "God, this is so hard, and I feel drained every moment and depleted, but I willingly give you this sacrifice, because you are worthy. I give you this sacrifice because of the reward you promise for my obedience", God can meet you and help you mother in His strength, which is unlimited!

If you keep praying and giving your obedient sacrifice, daily caring for the children the Lord has given you, teaching them His word, training them in the way they should go, and humbling yourself to the process with faith, then bit by bit you will find joy in the work and you will recognize the rewards along the way.

The rewards are big, and the rewards are in everyday small things that can easily be missed if you don't pay attention! A few that come to mind for me: My second son finding flowers to bring me every time he went outside when he was a toddler; my daughter holding and rocking her little sister and showing her so much love; to my oldest son, who declared at three years old that he will follow Jesus when he is a grown up. All these things, big and small are blessings and rewards for my labor in my house.

I give myself in service in my home, and God leads and guides me. I have faith that I will reap a great harvest from my willing labor if I do not faint if I do not give up.

2 Corinthians 12:9

And he said unto me, My grace is sufficient for thee: for my strength is made perfect in weakness. Most gladly therefore will I rather glory in my infirmities, that the power of Christ may rest upon me.

Hebrews 11:6

But without faith it is impossible to please him: for he that cometh to God must believe that he is, and that he is a rewarder of them that diligently seek him.

Matthew 11:28–29

Come unto me, all ye that labour and are heavy laden, and I will give you rest.
Take my yoke upon you, and learn of me; for I am meek and lowly in heart: and ye shall find rest unto your souls.

Galatians 6:8–10

For he that soweth to his flesh shall of the flesh reap corruption; but he that soweth to the Spirit shall of the Spirit reap life everlasting.

And let us not be weary in well doing: for in due season we shall reap, if we faint not.

As we have therefore opportunity, let us do good unto all men, especially unto them who are of the household of faith.

Romans 12:1

I beseech you therefore, brethren, by the mercies of God, that ye present your bodies a living sacrifice, holy, acceptable unto God, which is your reasonable service

PRAYER

Abba Father, I am grateful that I can come to you and find rest, grace, and strength in my weakness. God, I present my body to you as I serve my family. You are worthy of it.

I praise you and trust that as I surrender to you, you will give me joy and peace as I serve my family daily with your strength and power. I thank you for the future of peace and blessing that will come from my obedient sacrifice today. In the name of your son, Yeshua I pray. Amen.

Resist The Urge to Complain

*There are rewards for being a mother in God's kingdom, but
complaining and a sour attitude can make them unrecognizable to you.*

One night for Bible time with the children I just let the Bible fall
open to find something to read. It fell open on James 5. After skim-
ming the chapter, I found verse 9. It stood out to me on the page.

James 5:9 Grudge not one against another, brethren, lest ye be
condemned: behold, the judge standeth before the door.

Complaining and grumbling against your brethren in Christ
will bring you into condemnation, and God stands at the door ready
to judge those who complain and grumble.

Your children are no different. If you complain and grumble
against them, it will bring you into condemnation and judgement.
What an amazing revelation! It shook my soul.

I spent a lot of time trying to fight against complaining. This
Scripture gave me an urgent reason to not just fight against grumbling and complaining, but to totally resist it so it would flee from
me. There are rewards for being a mother in God's kingdom but complaining and a sour attitude can make them unrecognizable to you.

Pray for a cheerful heart and a thankful attitude. Then your eyes
will be able to see the rewards and blessings of motherhood. Meditate
on these scriptures, and keep in mind today that your children are
blessings from the Lord.

Philippians 2:13–15

For it is God which worketh in you both to will and to do of his good pleasure.

Do all things without murmurings and disputings:

That ye may be blameless and harmless, the sons of God, without rebuke, in the midst of a crooked and perverse nation, among whom ye shine as lights in the world;

Psalm 113:9

He maketh the barren woman to keep house, and to be a joyful mother of children. Praise ye the Lord.

Proverbs 10:22

The blessing of the Lord, it maketh rich, and he addeth no sorrow with it

PRAYER

Abba Father, you are the make and giver of life! Thank you for the life you have allowed me to birth into the earth. Lord, you have caused me to keep house, and I confess that I am a JOYFUL, mother of children.

The children you have given me make me rich and will not add sorrow to me. Lord, I look to you, you are my reward and I thank you for giving me eyes to see the blessings and rewards from my work in my home with my family. In the name of your son, Yeshua I pray. Amen.

Mother with Faith

Believe what you can't see.

All the seeds we plant as mothers seem small, but continue to walk in faith, believing that God will bring the increase to the love, time, teaching, and encouragement that you plant in your children. Believe what you can't see.

Hebrews 11:1

Now faith is the substance of things hoped for, the evidence of things not seen

When I was a brand-new mother, I went through a terrible bout of post-partum depression. We did not yet know about the hormone balancing effects of pre-natal vitamins and that women should continue to take them for a year post-partum. We did not know that a lack of vitamin D leads to depression. We did not yet understand these things, or why I was feeling so depressed for so long.

During that time, I saw my baby and realized that although he was an infant, he also had a living soul. So even though I was sad and depressed, I came up with a daily routine for him that included prayer and Bible time.

He was about three months old, and I would sit and read the Bible to him daily. My husband didn't quite understand why, but I continued because I felt like it was important for the word to be read aloud for his soul to hear and absorb, even if he did not understand.

As our baby grew into a toddler, my husband began to teach him the word as well. We would sing, pray, and read the Bible with him regularly. Esosa and I also would discuss the word together in front of him. We took him to church services and prayer meetings with us.

When he was two years old, he came to me and said Mommy, I want to go to heaven. I asked him questions and tried to understand what he was talking about. He was saying when it was time, he wanted to be able to go to heaven, not hell. I talked to him about what that meant and how Jesus died on the cross for him to be able to go to heaven.

My husband and I talked to him and explained to him what it meant to be saved. He said he wanted to receive Jesus and be saved. We led him in prayer and our two-year-old became a born-again believer.

Faith that God's word would transform our son's life bore fruit. We planted and watered seeds and God gave the increase. There are so many ways in which this principle can be applied in motherhood.

Sowing seeds of love, faith, a positive attitude, confident words, seeds of compassion, and joyfulness are all ways you can impact your child and provide the framework for God to move in their hearts. You may not feel happy or confident every time you do it. However, it is all done by faith. It takes time to see the fruit, but you will reap if you do not quit!

Psalms 126:5–6

⁵ *They that sow in tears shall reap in joy.* ⁶ *He that goeth forth and weepeth, bearing precious seed, shall doubtless come again with rejoicing, bringing his sheaves with him.*

Matthew 19:13–15

Then were there brought unto him little children, that he should put his hands on them, and pray: and the disciples rebuked them.

But Jesus said, Suffer little children, and forbid them not, to come unto me: for of such is the kingdom of heaven.

And he laid his hands on them, and departed thence.

PRAYER

Abba Father, my children are so precious to me, and I know they are even more precious to you. God, please use me in their lives and help me to plant and water good seeds on good ground in their hearts.

My faith is in you to bring the increase and transform their hearts and minds. Let the seeds of love, the teaching, and the word I plant in them bring forth much fruit and let me live to see it. In the name of your son, Yeshua I pray. Amen.

See It Now

Have strength of sight to see what you can't see.

See it now. See your snack-loving, giggling, running, tumbling bundles of joy as God-loving, successful men and women. See them someday building families of their own. This is what you are working for. This is the goal. Remember it and keep your head up. Have strength of sight to see what you can't see.

I recently heard another mom say, "the days are long, but the years are short". The days feel long while taking care of small children...but let's remember that the years go by so quickly.

Children are arrows in your hand and arrows in your quiver. It is your job to point them in the direction they are to make their mark and have impact. Point them in the direction they are to go spiritually and naturally. This should be our focus as mothers: sharpening, pointing, and releasing them in the direction they should go. How exciting to partner with God on such an important mission!

One day, that toddler at your leg will be a pastor leading God's sheep. One day, that little girl playing dress up and throwing her clothes all over her room will be witnessing for Christ on her college campus. One day, that boy asking questions non-stop will be a top engineer in his field, and a husband and father leading a family of his own. Let us be diligent to plant the right seeds and point them in the right direction in our daily interactions, so when it is time to release our arrows, they make their mark and hit on target in every area of their lives.

In the midst of the busyness, chaos, emotions, and schedules we have to fight to keep our eyes on what lies ahead.

Mothers must have vision to see what they can't see, so they are careful to plant the right seeds in the right seasons. When that toddler is a man, and that five-year-old princess is a woman, they have the strength, confidence, and foundation in Christ to build and be all that God has equipped them to.

You, woman of God, are building the future by investing your life and love into your children every day.

1 Corinthians 13:11

When I was a child, I spake as a child, I understood as a child, I thought as a child: but when I became a man, I put away childish things.

Zechariah 4:10a

For who hath despised the day of small things?

Psalm 127:4–5

As arrows are in the hand of a mighty man; so are children of the youth.
Happy is the man that hath his quiver full of them: they shall not be ashamed, but they shall speak with the enemies in the gate.

Proverbs 22:6

Train up a child in the way he should go: and when he is old, he will not depart from it

PRAYER

Abba Father, I thank you for giving me faith and vision for my children, and the future you have for them. Help me to see them now as the men and women you will make them.

God, please speak to me about my children, and let my confidence be in you that what you have created my children for will come to pass by your might and power. In the name of your son, Yeshua I pray. Amen.

Begin with The End in Mind

However you want your grandchildren to be treated,
is how you need to treat your children.

Imagine this scenario: A grandmother pops over to her son's house for a surprise visit and overhears her son yelling at her granddaughter. She puts her ears to the front door and listens in. As she stands there for what seems forever, her heart begins to break, flashbacks come to her mind of when her son was young and she used to yell at him.

Tears start to flow; she knows she can't bust in there and set him straight. He is the man of his own house now. She hurries and gets in her car and drives away before anyone notices she is there. She goes home to repent and pray and ask God for help on how to handle this.

This is the reality of generational abuse, whether it's mental, emotional, or physical. A lot of children who are yelled at, grow into yellers. A lot of children who are abused, grow into abusers.

Some people who were hurt or neglected by parents want to change and do better. Some struggle to do better because the negative words and examples that were set for them surface when they are raising their own children.

We have all made mistakes in parenting, but today is a new day and God's mercy is brand new for all of us.

Reflect on your overall attitude as a mother. Are you mostly kind and patient or short-tempered and irritated? When your child spills or drops something, are you quick to react in anger, or do you patiently set them at ease and let them know it's ok it was a mistake? Do you find yourself yelling at your child? Or dealing with their misbehavior with loving correction?

Examine yourself, pray, and ask God to show you what needs to improve in your parenting. Your future grandchildren are depending on you to set a good example and bless them with a loving and kind mommy or daddy.

Galatians 6:7–8

Be not deceived; God is not mocked: for whatsoever a man soweth, that shall he also reap.

For he that soweth to his flesh shall of the flesh reap corruption; but he that soweth to the Spirit shall of the Spirit reap life everlasting.

1 Corinthians 13:4–7

Charity suffereth long, and is kind; charity envieth not; charity vaunteth not itself, is not puffed up,

Doth not behave itself unseemly, seeketh not her own, is not easily provoked, thinketh no evil;

Rejoiceth not in iniquity, but rejoiceth in the truth;

Beareth all things, believeth all things, hopeth all things, endureth all things.

PRAYER

Abba Father, please forgive me of ways that I have hurt or damaged my child and our relationship. Lord, I want to be a good mother, but I cannot do it in my own strength. Please heal me of all the abuse and trauma of my own childhood.

I forgive my parents for ways they have hurt me. God, please stop all generational curses, and let them proceed no further. Bless me, make me whole, and help me to be a mother that raises children who are well loved and able to love their own children well. In the name of your son, Yeshua I pray. Amen.

The Power is in The Love

*Honor your husband and children by serving them
with LOVE, not frustration or anger.*

There are so many responsibilities that come along with being a wife and a mother. So many expectations; so much we have to give.

Early mornings, late nights, sleepless nights, endless cooking, a never-ending list of things that need to be cleaned, and piles and piles of laundry. Investing in our marriage, supporting our husbands, training, and supporting the children.

The Proverbs 31 responsibility can feel overwhelming to say the least. However, being wife and mother is also a place of great honor and a position of great influence. My mother used to say that it was a position of power. How? How is constantly serving the needs of a family a position of power?

As the wife, you have the ability to influence your husband in your attitude, lifestyle, and relationship with Christ. You have the power to help him feel empowered with your words of encouragement, with your prayers, and by helping him live out the purpose God has given him.

With the children, you have the power to build up their confidence, influence the way they act and treat others, and ultimately you are anointed by God to train them into what God has called them to be. Oh, yes, you have a great position of power.

With the potential of power and influence you hold with the people in your family, how then should you serve and live this out?

How should you carry such a great and honorable calling? With Love. Showing love, giving love, and serving with love daily. Honor your husband and children by serving them with LOVE, not frustration or anger.

Is it easy to do it in love? No. Is it possible? Most definitely. It is not easy because we have to fight against ourselves in order to serve with love and humility.

What about me? What about what I want? What about my plans, my career, my business?

Well, those things are important, but the prioritized goal now is to build a Godly household, founded upon the rock of Christ Jesus. All other goals must now shift to support this primary goal. If they do not support this goal, then they need to be eliminated.

Once you have your priorities in line, it is much easier to serve your family in love. Feeling like your family is a barrier to your career, business, or personal happiness is a major obstacle to serving in love. You have to see your family as a top priority over other things in order to do it in love every day.

Overcoming your own emotions is another must on your journey of serving with love. Training yourself to think on good things is crucial. The pressure of so many responsibilities can feel weighty at times.

Your heart can feel tired and your capacity can be stretched to the limit. Frustration, anger, depression, negative thinking, and speaking can all try and creep up on your mind.

The key to overcoming is realizing that satan wants to steal, kill, and destroy everyone in your household. What better way for him to get to your family, his target of destruction, than through you, the one with deep connections to everyone in the house?

What you have to realize is you do not want to be a tool of the devil against your own family!

Marrying someone then tearing them down? Going through hours of labor to give birth to a child, then tearing them down with your words, actions, and example? What a waste of time, money, energy, and your life!

This is why the Bible says a wise woman builds her house, and a foolish woman plucks it down with her hands (Proverbs 14:1). It is so foolish to invest so much into people, while simultaneously destroying them.

Mount up woman of God and put on strength.

Mount up woman of God and put on Love.

Mount up woman of God and let the LAW OF KINDNESS be in your tongue.

Serving a family is a position of great power and you have the ability to do it in love, through Christ Jesus.

Cook in love, clean with a spirit of love, do the laundry in love, play with your children in love, serve your husband in love, encourage, build, and motivate in love.

If you are able to overcome your flesh, overcome the devil, and let love shine in your household, how great is your reward?

But if you cave into your feelings, cave into anger, and open the door to the destroyer through your anger and bitterness, what devastation will rain down.

Not only on your family, but future generations as well.

Matthew 23:10–12

Neither be ye called masters: for one is your Master, even Christ.

But he that is greatest among you shall be your servant.

And whosoever shall exalt himself shall be abased; and he that shall humble himself shall be exalted.

2 Corinthians 13:14

The grace of the Lord Jesus Christ, and the love of God, and the communion of the Holy Ghost, be with you all. Amen.

PRAYER

Abba Father, I thank you for my life and the family you have given me. I pray Lord, that the grace of the Lord Jesus, the love of God and communion with the Holy Spirit would be with me as I minister to them daily.

Lord God, You love my family. Help us to grow together in your love. In the name of your son, Yeshua I pray. Amen.

Love Under Pressure

Who you are when you discipline your child defines you as a mother.

Who are you when giving discipline? Angry and mean? Frustrated and discouraging?

How about administering discipline with patience, love, and kindheartedness? God help us to do so.

The last two years of my life have been extremely difficult. I lost my mother and gave birth to two stillborn baby girls from two different pregnancies. All of this happened within an 18-month period. To help cope with the immense losses, a friend and I started reading a book on grieving. The book does a great job of illustrating the sacrificial love of Christ. This helped me to realize how Jesus was really good at showing love under pressure.

Sometimes after He would preach, crowds would throng Him for healing. He loved. Sometimes when He was preaching, someone would ask Him for healing. After that healing, someone would need Him for something else. He loved. His disciples argued and were difficult to instruct. He loved.

Finally, when He was on the cross in unbearable pain, He prayed for those who hurt Him and also showed compassion on one of the criminals dying with Him. He LOVED. Christ experienced great pressure in all these situations, yet He showed love at all times, He WAS love at all times.

The intensity of the grief I was suffering made me feel entitled to melt downs, grumpiness, and losing my temper with my children. The force of the pain I was dealing with knocked the wind out of me to say the least, and some days I felt I could barely get out of bed. Was my pain justified? Most certainly. Three significant losses in less than two years can truly take a toll on a person's heart and life. Was I justified in taking my emotions out on my children? Most certainly not. The suffering of Christ was far greater than anything I could ever imagine, yet He managed to show love. If He did it through His pain, He could empower me to show love through mine.

The pressures we face in motherhood are intense but cannot compare with the pressures and sufferings of Christ. If He was able to overcome the suffering He faced and still show love, with the help of God, moms can too.

Matthew 9:18–33

While he spake these things unto them, behold, there came a certain ruler, and worshipped him, saying, My daughter is even now dead: but come and lay thy hand upon her, and she shall live.

And Jesus arose, and followed him, and so did his disciples.

And, behold, a woman, which was diseased with an issue of blood twelve years, came behind him, and touched the hem of his garment:

For she said within herself, If I may but touch his garment, I shall be whole.

But Jesus turned him about, and when he saw her, he said, Daughter, be of good comfort; thy faith hath made thee whole. And the woman was made whole from that hour.

And when Jesus came into the ruler's house, and saw the minstrels and the people making a noise,

He said unto them, Give place: for the maid is not dead, but sleepeth. And they laughed him to scorn.

But when the people were put forth, he went in, and took her by the hand, and the maid arose.

And the fame hereof went abroad into all that land.

And when Jesus departed thence, two blind men followed him, crying, and saying, Thou son of David, have mercy on us.

And when he was come into the house, the blind men came to him: and Jesus saith unto them, Believe ye that I am able to do this? They said unto him, Yea, Lord.

Then touched he their eyes, saying, According to your faith be it unto you.

And their eyes were opened; and Jesus straitly charged them, saying, See that no man know it.

But they, when they were departed, spread abroad his fame in all that country.

As they went out, behold, they brought to him a dumb man possessed with a devil.

And when the devil was cast out, the dumb spake: and the multitudes marvelled, saying, It was never so seen in Israel.

PRAYER

Abba Father, you are good and mighty and powerful. There is none like you, Lord. Jesus ministered to many and was loving and kind.

Help me Lord, to meet the needs of my family with the grace of the Lord Jesus. Help me to do all things in love with the grace and favor of God. Thank you for the example that Christ has set for me. In the name of your son, Yeshua I pray. Amen.

Choose The Good Parts

Let your heart relax and feel the love of your family.

Motherhood is a lot of work. And there is a temptation to zone in on the to-do list, because honestly, there is a lot to do! However, we must fight and keep ourselves from being so focused on how much work there is that we don't take the time to enjoy being together. Let your heart relax and feel the love of your family.

"People over productivity." This was a word God spoke to me when I was pregnant with my second child. My oldest was barely one years old. God was preparing me for life with a toddler and newborn, both in diapers.

I would need to learn to focus on the people I was caring for instead of focusing on checking things off my to-do list. I would no longer be able to measure my productivity by the tasks I completed, rather the people I ministered to.

Look past the laundry on the couch that needs to be folded, the dishes that may need to be washed, put your phone away in a drawer and look at the beautiful faces of your children and just breathe.

There is always something to do, wash, cook, and clean. But the faces you see will be all grown up one day. So, embrace them and let your heart relax and feel love for them, and not just responsibility for them.

This can be hard, especially if you have many children. One thing I try to remind myself of is that the house is here for us, and we are not here for the house, the clothing, food, etc. It is all here to support our family. The things should not be the priority, the people are. It is hard to feel the joy in a relationship when all you can do is focus on the responsibility of it. Just feel the joy of your children being in your presence and let that fill your heart.

I have the tendency to be like Martha in the story of sisters, Martha and Mary found in Luke chapter 10. The sisters were hosting Jesus and His disciples at their house. Martha was busy with much serving, while her sister Mary was sitting at Jesus feet. Martha asked Jesus to make her sister get up and help with the work. Jesus told Martha that Mary had chosen the better part, sitting at His feet and being in His presence.

Now of course our children do not compare to Christ in any way. The connection I am making is that Mary had chosen the better part, to be caught up in fellowship and communion of a relationship, not focused and stressed about the work.

Being a mother is your opportunity to do fun things with your child. You have an opportunity to spend time with your child, and give your child/children plenty of love, attention, affection, and encouragement.

We do have pressures and responsibilities in life that can affect the quality of our parenting if we let it. But with humility and prayer, God can show you how to minister to each of your children, and help you find the time to pour into their lives on a regular basis.

Managing our responsibilities in a way that will allow us to spend a maximum amount of time with your children is a fight we must all engage in. It is a worthy fight, and one worth winning. A close bond and relationship with your child is the great reward of winning this battle.

If the pressures of housework and the daily care of your children does not cause you to be distracted and stressed, think about something that does and make that the focus of your prayer for peace.

Luke 10:38–42

Now it came to pass, as they went, that he entered into a certain village: and a certain woman named Martha received him into her house.

And she had a sister called Mary, which also sat at Jesus' feet, and heard his word.

But Martha was cumbered about much serving, and came to him, and said, Lord, dost thou not care that my sister hath left me to serve alone? bid her therefore that she help me.

And Jesus answered and said unto her, Martha, Martha, thou art careful and troubled about many things:

But one thing is needful: and Mary hath chosen that good part, which shall not be taken away from her.

PRAYER

Abba Father, I thank you for the love, grace, and mercy that you show me daily. Thank you for keeping my family in my hands Father. I worship you as the only living God.

Lord, there are so many things to be troubled about, so many things that I feel needs to be done. But Lord, being in constant relationship and fellowship with you is most important, followed by pouring love into those around me. God, help me to choose the one thing that is needful, and trust you. In the name of your son, Yeshua, I pray. Amen.

Have Love for Yourself

God, please help me to depend on you to meet my
needs as I freely pour love out on my children.

As most mothers know, it can be difficult to meet the constant needs of your children and take care of your own needs on a regular basis. While you are serving them, providing appropriate discipline, encouragement, washing their laundry, cooking their meals, combing their hair, and having play sessions with them, it can feel next to impossible to take proper care of yourself, physically, emotionally, and spiritually.

This is where we reach out to God and cast our care upon Him, knowing that He cares for us. Caring for yourself is part of caring for your family. It took me years to realize that I am part of the family and I need to be cared for like everyone else.

As I make sure my children are fed spiritually, I also need to be fed spiritually. I make sure they look good, so I need to make sure I look good. I make sure they have activities and opportunities to exercise, so I need to make time to exercise. I make sure they are growing and developing mentally; I need to ensure that I am growing and developing mentally as well. I must love my neighbor as I love myself. This is the second commandment!

As God gives you a way to meet your needs, He may give you ideas on how to schedule time for yourself. He will help you to care for the different needs you have as a person as you continue to care for your children.

He may send you a friend to workout with, He may bless you with extra money to buy the new clothes you need, or bless you with a bit of extra time before the children get up in the morning to get in the Word, etc. When you pray, make sure you are open to the ways He may answer your prayer, and respond to the answers when He sends them.

The Lord is so faithful. Another way to ensure you are caring for yourself, is to incorporate your self-care into your care for the children, and vice-versa. Instead of the children feeling like a hinderance to your exercise time, incorporate them into it! I work out with my children often. Sometimes, it may be a workout with the whole family, or just the girls and I, or I might lift weights with my boys and husband. Sometimes, I take walks with the children or we have walks as a family. The possibilities are endless.

Sure, our family workouts flow a lot differently than when I work out alone, but our group workouts are fun. It teaches them good habits and shows a healthy example for them to follow when they are adults. Win-win!

When I need to wash my hair, sometimes I do a wash day with the girls. I spend the day washing all our hair and talking to them about how to care for their hair when they are older. Win-win!

The girls and I do our nails together sometimes, also. Of course, there are times when you need to get away and have alone time. But, finding a way to care for yourself as you care for your children will help you to be more consistent in whatever routine or schedule you set for self-care.

The fact that Jesus is God in the flesh and still very practical and easy to identify with, is amazing to me. Jesus had multitudes of people following Him that He ministered to at times. A group of disciples he was leading constantly. But get this, He also got away by himself. Just Him and His Father. He did that.

Jesus was all about His purpose on the earth and recognized His need to be alone in the presence of God. Woman of God, there is wisdom in getting away when you need to. You are important to your family, which is more reason to find time to be alone and gather your thoughts.

That time may look different for everyone and the amount of time may look different for everyone. The point is, rest is good, time alone with God is good and will hopefully be restful for your soul.

Mark 6:30–32

And the apostles gathered themselves together unto Jesus, and told him all things, both what they had done, and what they had taught.

And he said unto them, Come ye yourselves apart into a desert place, and rest a while: for there were many coming and going, and they had no leisure so much as to eat.

And they departed into a desert place by ship privately.

Luke 5:16

And he withdrew himself into the wilderness, and prayed.

PRAYER

Abba Father, I thank you for your thoughtfulness towards us. Thank you that you care about all that concerns us. Please teach me Lord how to care for my family and find time to care for myself and spend time alone with you. Yahuah, please help me to depend on you to meet my needs as I freely pour love out on my children and family.

You mean so much to me, and I can do nothing without you. Give me wisdom and teach me how to structure our family schedule so we can all get what we need. In the name of your son, Yeshua I pray. Amen.

Practical Thanksgivings

Be grateful!

Everything may not be perfect, but there is so much to be thankful for. It is easy to get overly focused on the problem areas in our lives, that we can lose sight of all the things that are going well and the progress we are making.

Learning to be thankful will also train you to think on good things and also communicates to the Most High God, that you appreciate what He has blessed you with.

Thankfulness is also a great example to your children.

Sometimes when we have family prayer, we will all go around and say three things that we are thankful for. Other times, we may have a praise session where we praise and sing to Yah. Other times, quietly to myself I will thank God for His blessings, when I feel the temptation to complain creeping up.

Make a written list of 10 things concerning your children that you are grateful for today.

Think on these things and give verbal praise to God for these things ALL DAY LONG!

Here are ten verses to help you!

1. *Ephesians 5:20—Giving thanks always for all things unto God and the Father in the name of our Lord Jesus Christ;*
2. *1 Thessalonians 5:18—In everything give thanks: for this is the will of God in Christ Jesus concerning you.*
3. *Psalms 106:1—Praise ye the LORD. O give thanks unto the LORD; for [he is] good: for his mercy [endureth] forever.*
4. *Philippians 4:6—Be careful for nothing; but in every-thing by prayer and supplication with thanksgiving let your requests be made known unto God.*
5. *Psalms 107:1—O give thanks unto the LORD, for [he is] good: for his mercy [endureth] forever.*
6. *Psalms 100:4—Enter into his gates with thanksgiving, [and] into his courts with praise: be thankful unto him, [and] bless his name.*
7. *Colossians 3:15–17—And let the peace of God rule in your hearts, to the which also ye are called in one body; and be ye thankful.*
8. *Colossians 4:2—Continue in prayer, and watch in the same with thanksgiving;*
9. *Psalms 28:7—The LORD [is] my strength and my shield; my heart trusted in him, and I am helped: therefore my heart greatly rejoiceth; and with my song will I praise him.*
10. *1 Thessalonians 1:2—We give thanks to God always for you all, making mention of you in our prayers;*

PRAYER

Abba Father, I thank you so much for all that you have given me. You are so good and kind to me. Thank you for my children, thank you for the ability to love, care for, and raise them to fear you God.

God, I praise you, help me to do all things with love and for your glory. All things are yours and I praise you for what you have entrusted me with. In the name of your son, Yashua I pray. Amen.

Order Brings The Glory of God to Your Family

Although you are Mom and very connected to your babies, Dad has a special place of authority in your child's life and a position given by God.

It is critical for every mother to understand how detrimental it is to cast aside input, suggestions, and decisions that Dad makes. Your child needs him and his guidance, maybe more than you know.

Fathers are immeasurably important in the life of a child. Fathers have an innate ability from God to provide leadership and guidance in the lives of their children. Unfortunately, in the rage of feminism our culture has lost sight of that.

Even in the kingdom of God, we have in many ways lost sight of the position a father plays in the family, society, and the church. However, God is restoring the order in family and once again placing men at the head of it.

Women can be so instrumental in this if we through humility, support the husband & father as he leads, instead of challenging him.

When a child observes you being respectful and obedient to your husband, it teaches them how they are to also relate to their father. When the child learns to respect their father, the father is able to give guidance and instruction to them and have the child follow and obey.

This brings order to families and to the church.

As women, we do not honor husband/fathers as leaders when they become perfect. We honor them as leaders in our homes because it is a position given to them by the Most High.

We cannot change it. You actually bring a blessing on your home and in the lives of your children when you obey the order Yah has set.

If you teach your children directly or indirectly to disobey their father, eventually they will begin to disobey you as well.

Children gain character and grow in Godliness when they learn to obey their father and follow his counsel and guidance. Their father is their crown.

How do we address the fact that some fathers are ungodly and give bad advice at some times?

In 1 Samuel 25, Scripture gives us the account of Abigail. She was married to a fool named Nabal. Even his name meant "fool" in Hebrew. However, his wife Abigail was wise. The way she respected, honored, and tried to protect her foolish husband is a good example for all women with ungodly husbands.

It is very unwise to dishonor your husband, or the father of your children. Unless he is telling you to violate God's commandments, it's best to follow his instruction and advice.

A wise woman supports and helps her husband, and lets her husband learn leadership and decision-making without stealing it from him. Let God be the one to lead him or punish his foolishness, not you.

Limiting your husband's leadership will only limit the glory of your children. The higher you push your husband, the higher your children will rise.

> **Proverbs 17:6 Children's children are the crown of old men; and the glory of children are their fathers.**

PRAYER

Abba Father, I thank you for the order you have created in the family. Your wisdom is higher than ours. Yahuah, I humble myself before you and I ask that you create in me a clean heart and renew a right spirit within me, that I may obey your order. I ask that you would give me to strength to lead my children in honoring, respecting and obeying their father. All things are possible with you. In the name of your son Yeshua I pray, Amen.

Training for Reigning

*Faith that your children are called and chosen
by God will change how you mother.*

Every person is made in God's image and has a purpose. A child is a future adult. A boy is a future husband, father, warrior, and servant leader. A girl is a future wife, mother, nurturer, and virtuous and powerful woman.

The way you train them, teach them, talk to them, and discipline them are tools you are putting in their tool box for them to use when they are in positions of leadership.

Wow, let that soak in.

Your treatment of them is training for how they will treat others and also how they will think about and present themselves. It is a sobering thought for me for sure.

Another thing to ponder is that children are special and precious to God. Oh, how some seem to have forgotten that. The word says that the angels of children always behold the face of God.

> *Matthew 18:10 Take heed that ye despise not one of these little ones; for I say unto you, That in heaven their angels do always behold the face of my Father which is in heaven.*

Once when Jesus was teaching, some people came to Him with their children. His disciples tried to turn them away, but what did Jesus say? Some may know this passage by heart, "Suffer little children to come unto me and forbid them not; for of such is the kingdom of heaven" (Matthew 19:14).

Jesus loves and embraces children, He loved on them when He walked the earth, and He loves them now. God can pour out so much on our children that we must be sensitive to His leading.

Read the word of God with them daily and discuss it. Pray with them earnestly and taking their questions to God when you do not have an answer. These are all ways to help them develop in their relationship with God.

Your child is called by God. How can you position them to receive an outpouring of God's Spirit? How can you teach them to study God's word?

As parents, we are concerned about our children's education, social interactions and future career. But something that needs even more attention in their growth and development is helping them become disciples of Christ.

We need to help them learn to truth of God's word more and more. The Bible instructs us to teach children His ways. There is a scripture that instructs parents to teach your children of Him at all times during the day.

Deuteronomy 11:18–20

Therefore shall ye lay up these my words in your heart and in your soul, and bind them for a sign upon your hand, that they may be as frontlets between your eyes.

And ye shall teach them your children, speaking of them when thou sittest in thine house, and when thou walkest by the way, when thou liest down, and when thou risest up.

And thou shalt write them upon the door posts of thine house, and upon thy gates:

PRAYER

Abba Father, you have created my children and given them pur-pose. I praise you because they are fearfully and wonderfully made. Yah, I call out to you and I ask that you would help me to see them for who you created them to be. Help me to teach and train them in the way they should go, for what you have created them for.

I pray that I would possess the love, peace, joy, and vision nec-essary to help them become who and what you created them to be. Let the grace of the Lord Jesus, the love of God and communion with the Holy Spirit be with them in the name of your son, Yeshua I pray. Amen.

Do Not Despise The Days of Small Beginnings

The time when your children are small is an opportunity to take their hearts.

When your children are small, they want to be with you constantly; talking to you and playing with you. This is the Lord's opportunity to build trust and closeness so that when they are older, you can be a trusted source of love, guidance and counsel. The time when your children are small is an opportunity to take their hearts.

Patiently teach, train, love, and enjoy your little ones, so that you will be the one they come to when they are young adults needing life-changing guidance.

The call of "Moooommyyyyyy!!!" while you are in the middle of folding laundry, washing the dishes, or working in your office does not always make your heart leap for joy.

It can be very challenging to lovingly meet the needs and demands of small children, while managing all your other duties and responsibilities. Trust me, I know.

Over the years, I have come to realize those little hands reaching up for me, those little feet following me around the house, constantly being invited to play cars, trains, or build with playdough are actually one of the greatest opportunities I have to impact the world and the kingdom of God.

If mothers take the time, and patiently love on, engage with, and pour into that little one, you have the potential to build a bond that will help you become a trusted confidante as they grow and mature… as they become the leaders of the next generation.

The wrong response to your child's need for you can cause them to distrust you, and can fracture your relationship with them. It can make them feel isolated and displaced and alone in their own home.

It always goes back to trusting God to meet your needs as you meet theirs. Asking God to strengthen you to meet the demand, and also serving them in humility, with love, as unto the Lord. They won't be that young forever; they will grow, change, develop, and leave home one day Lord willing. But you want them leaving home with confidence, hopefulness, and joy in their hearts.

Nurturing and reassuring mothering from a Godly mother can help lay that foundation, and it all starts with your attitude and the love with which you serve them and interact with the now.

So Sis, let the joy of the Lord be your strength as you love, serve, and serve, and serve. You will be rewarded with loving relationships with your children if you walk in the fruits of the spirit towards them, even when the demands are hard to meet.

You CAN do it, if you rely on the One who's strength is made perfect in your weakness.

Proverbs 15:1

A soft answer turneth away wrath: but grievous words stir up anger

Proverbs 23:26

My son, give me thine heart, and let thine eyes observe my ways.

Proverbs 22:6

Train up a child in the way he should go: and when he is old, he will not depart from it.

PRAYER

Abba Father, I thank you for my children, thank you for rewarding me with them. Please teach me how to meet the demands of motherhood with the love and joy that only comes from your Spirit.

Heavenly Father, You are a good Father, loving, kind and faithful, help me to be like you as I parent my children. In the name of your son Yeshua I pray. Amen.

Relax and Enjoy!

Do the best you can every day. Thank God, trust God and enjoy life!

I never understood how to rest and work (resting in God and working in purpose) without stress.

My aha moment came to me one night as I was talking with my husband after an exhausting week of nonstop work. Despite my best efforts, the house was still a mess.

At the time my boys were six months, 2 years old and 3 years old. As we walked and talked, this word came out of my mouth. "This is how you work with a restful spirit: do your best, thank God no matter what, trust God for everything, and just enjoy the life He has given you!"

Amen.

Mommy life can feel nonstop when you are in the thick of it and your children are young. A friend of mine who has seven children, and I were talking together. I mentioned to her that we were open to receive all the children God wanted to give us. She looked at me with a very stern face and said, "I hope you are ready, with an energizer battery in your back!" I laughed; it was a very funny comment. At the time I was pregnant with my fourth child.

However, a few short years later I realized what she said was not a joke! Once I had five children, I felt like I was spinning around my house like a top!

I am the first to confess what the Bible says, children are a BLESSING! And I also acknowledge that raising children can be difficult and bring the strongest person to their knees.

The key to finding the strength to balance the blessing with the workload is found in the word of God, but isn't that always the case?

The key is disciplining your emotions and training yourself to cast your burdens and cares upon the Lord, daily, hourly, or minute by minute (sometimes it's second-by-second)!

Also, the time when your children are young is not the time to expect everything to be perfect in your home, schedule, routines, etc. It is not an excuse to be lazy, but just keep your goals in perspective, ask for help, and have grace on yourself.

You do not want to spend these precious years in a ball of stress over things that will not matter AT ALL twenty years from now. What will matter twenty years from now, is the time, love of God, and word of God that you invest in your children.

Another important element in learning to work from a place of rest is allowing God to strengthen you for the task, instead of shrinking back.

Proverbs 31 tells us that a virtuous woman strengthens herself for the task. Allowing God to strengthen you for the work of raising your family, will give you rest, because your capacity (what you can do and handle) will level up and you won't feel so overwhelmed.

This requires a humbling to the work and seeking God on how to do and go about things. As He reveals answers, submit, despite how you feel. Before long, things that used to be hard and stressful to you, you will be able to do with peace.

Spending all your time complaining will only make things feel harder and harder. You will not learn, grow, or expand your capacity at the rate you should and it will be difficult to mature.

Woman of God, please know, that as I minister to you, the word is also ministering to me. For we are all continually being perfected as Christ completes the work He has started in us.

Work with a restful heart and be happy. Do your work with love and be happy with all that you did accomplish during the day, instead of dwelling on all that did not get done.

I know this can be difficult for us, but trust me, it will save you stress and free your mind to ENJOY your family more, instead of feeling so burdened by your work.

Philippians 4:8

Finally, brethren, whatsoever things are true, whatsoever things are honest, whatsoever things are just, whatsoever things are pure, whatsoever things are lovely, whatsoever things are of good report; if there be any virtue, and if there be any praise, think on these things.

1 Peter 5:6–8

Humble yourselves therefore under the mighty hand of God, that he may exalt you in due time:
Casting all your care upon him; for he careth for you.
Be sober, be vigilant; because your adversary the devil, as a roaring lion, walketh about, seeking whom he may devour:

PRAYER

Abba Father, thank you so much for the beauty of family. Truly your wisdom is higher than ours and your ways are past finding out. Lord God, I humble myself before you. I can do nothing of my own strength, but I can only do this work by your power and your Holy Spirit. God, please help me to do good work that is pleasing in your sight.

Help me Father, to cast my care and burdens upon you, you care for me and only you can carry our family where we need to be always. So, I put my trust in you and I rest from worry. Give me joy in motherhood in the name of your son Yeshua I pray. Amen.

Embrace the Changes

*They are your children, they love you, challenge you,
mature you. Let them make you better!*

Well, God has done it again. As I type this, I have had quite the day with my bunch of little olive plants. Writing on this topic for you is right on time. Most of my children had a tough day behaving and following directions. They challenged me for sure!

Amen Lord, I will let them make me better. Today, what that means for me is allowing their challenging behavior to help me level up in choosing peace and resisting the temptation to walk in anger even when their behavior makes me upset.

Sometimes, it is hard to do. Praying out loud in moments of stress has been helping a lot. I've been talking to God, releasing the problems to Him. Today, I had to give everyone a nap, even my older ones, so we could all take a breather.

Allow the challenge of motherhood to make you better. Instead of running, instead of allowing anger to take over, instead of blaming the children, stand and find ways to grow. Ask the Holy Spirit to guide you in the situation you face with your miniature men and women of God.

You can find joy in the fact that your children are with you, and they love you. They sit on your lap because they love you, they follow you around the house because they love you, they ask to sleep with you because they love you, and they are always in your face because they love you, Sis! Embrace that love, and thank God for it; it is a gift.

Maturing into the role of motherhood is the stage I am in. Having a baby is one thing but stepping into the role of motherhood is totally different. It is marked by accepting and embracing the honor of your position in your child's life.

It is refusing to pass off the responsibilities of raising that child and refusing to neglect needs you see that your child has. It is becoming the nurturer, the kind voice, the place of reassurance, and the source of discipline your child needs as they go through the different phases of childhood. It is not forcing them to accept you as you are but changing and becoming what you need to be for their success, with God's help and the power of His word, and prayer. This is the Anointing of Motherhood.

> *1 Corinthians 9:19*
>
> *For though I be free from all men, yet have I made myself servant unto all, that I might gain the more*
>
> *Philippians 4:13*
>
> *I can do all things through Christ which strengtheneth me.*

PRAYER

Abba Father, thank you for your word. Thank you for the Holy Spirit that leads me into all truth. God, my children are blessings from you. Thank you for opening my eyes and heart, that I might embrace, enjoy, and take pleasure in the great blessing they are to me.

Please forgive me for the times I have been ungrateful and unthankful. Help me to become what you need me to be in the lives of my children Lord, that I might win them to Christ. Thank you for this work, in the name of your son Yeshua I pray. Amen.

Lead with Love

*Seek quality interactions with your children,
even when you discipline them.*

Your goal as a mother is for love to color your child's memories of home, and for love to shape their personality.

In all things as Christian mothers, we should be focused on making disciples of our children. It is much easier to teach someone and lead them in Christ when they are confident that your intentions come from a place of love.

With children, they may not use that language or be able to articulate it this way, but they can feel your love or lack thereof and it will show in how they respond to you. Always assure your children of your love, even when you are upset.

There are so many thoughts that go through a child's mind in a day. Questioning whether mommy loves them should not even be a thought in their minds.

After they are punished or corrected for a mistake is a very important time to reinforce the truth of your love and God's love for them. In the anger or frustration they feel when punished, the enemy can easily creep in and plant seeds of insecurity and discord in their hearts towards you.

Don't give the devil any room to convince your child you don't love them. Your words of love, acts of love, and embrace should be a constant reminder.

We should all spend time in prayer asking God how we can create a loving atmosphere in our home. It can look different for all of us since our families have different needs. But this is something God can lead you in and give you the ability to do.

Having a peaceful and loving home life can make all the difference in helping children develop Godly character and even affect their mental and emotional health, and academic performance.

Even in a loving home, conflict still needs to be resolved, and obedience to authority is still mandatory. That is a normal part of living with other people. What changes is how we resolve conflict and motivate obedience. Ask God in sincerity how to create a loving atmosphere in your home and how to deal with each conflict that arises. The Holy Spirit loves to lead us.

Jeremiah 31:3

The Lord hath appeared of old unto me, saying, Yea, I have loved thee with an everlasting love: therefore with lovingkindness have I drawn thee.

1 Peter 4:8

And above all things have fervent charity among yourselves: for charity shall cover the multitude of sins

PRAYER

Abba Father, You are an everlasting source of love and comfort and joy. By the blood of your son Jesus, I have been redeemed and am now your child. Help me Lord to love my children with your love and create an atmosphere of love in my home.

Teach us to communicate in love, encourage one another in love, spend time together in love, and resolve conflict I love. I pray that the grace of the Lord Jesus, and the love of God, and the comfort of the Holy Ghost would be with us all. In the name of your son, Yeshua I pray. Amen.

Release the Pressure. Possess the Peace

Release yourself to believe you are doing a good job.

Discouragement is a beast. Feeling downtrodden and down on yourself all the time is not a good recipe for self-improvement. Even if God shows you that you need to improve in some areas, or corrects you, that means He loves you and know you CAN do better, which is a cause to rejoice.

We all have our lingering to-do list, many things get crossed off, and a lot of things don't. Allowing yourself the space in your mind to focus on the things that you do or did well in your home and caring for your family, will help give courage to your heart to push and improve in other areas.

I have a perfectionist personality. I like things to be neat and orderly. This does not mix well with a house full of children! God has really had to teach me and change me in a lot of ways. It has been very hard for me to believe I am doing a good job, when so many things were so far from my standards.

However, my mother had a dream about me when I was a child. She never understood the dream, but I believe I have the interpretation now. She dreamed I was chasing a train trying to get on it. The train conductor would not stop the train for me and was very cruel.

Over the years, I have pondered this dream. As a woman and mother, I believe the interpretation of the dream is this: the train and conductor are perfection. I am chasing it but can never catch it. No matter how hard I run, I will never catch it.

Once God dropped that revelation in my spirit, I realized it was time to stop chasing it. Like I mentioned before, I need to do my best and be thankful in God's rest!

It is important that you access your personality and natural bend. Some people are too relaxed and careless with things, while others are too uptight and stressed about things. You don't want to be fall into either ditch. You want to be walking in the middle.

Doing all things as unto the Lord, working diligently with your hands, looking well after the ways of your household, while also taking God's yoke and burden which is easy and light. Sigh!!! What a relief!

If you get up every day allowing God to minister to your family through you, loving your husband and loving your children, and working in your house with diligence (diligence looks different at different stages of motherhood), you are doing a good job!

Be at peace as you allow God to grow and mature you and improve you in different ways. As He is perfecting you, grab hold of peace and think on good things.

Proverbs 18:14

The spirit of a man will sustain his infirmity; but a wounded spirit who can bear?

1 Samuel 30:6b

...but David encouraged himself in the Lord his God.

PRAYER

Abba Father, I know you love me. You showed your great love by sending your son Jesus to die on the cross for my sins and the sins of the world. You are almighty, gracious, powerful, and omniscient. I humble myself before you Lord and I ask that you would teach me how to encourage myself as your servant and as a mother.

Please strengthen my spirit man through your word and wisdom daily. Help me Lord to focus on the things that are truly important, so that everyone in our family will bear maximum fruit. In the name of your son, Yeshua I pray. Amen.

Play your Creation Role

"Whose body did I put the baby in? Whose body makes milk for the baby? So, who do you think is supposed to be the one primarily caring for the baby?"

These were God's words to me when I was crying and frustrated about feeling like the burden of caring for our first baby fell on me alone.

When I gave birth to our first child, I was not sure what I expected from my husband. But based on my emotional response, I suppose I was expecting to split the work, 50/50. Lol.

That was a far cry from reality. I do not recall how much, if any, time he had off work after the baby was born. I just remember that after a few weeks, his life seemed to go back to normal, while I felt like my freedom had been snuffed out. He was going to work, running errands, going to different events, and I was sitting at home.

Of course, he helped when he was home, but the care of the baby was mostly my responsibility. For some reason, that is not what I was expecting. I began to resent his ability to come and go as he pleased.

The first few months with your first child are a huge learning curve. The first few weeks for women are especially tough as her body recovers from giving birth. But after everything settled down and I was still sitting in the nest like a mother duck, I felt abandoned and like my life was over and I would never be able to go do anything again!

Dramatic? Sure! I was an emotional wreck after I had my first child. But through the emotions, the Lord spoke those words to me. "Whose body did I put the baby in? Whose body makes milk for the baby? So, who do you think is supposed to be the one primarily caring for the baby?"

What retort do you have against the wisdom of the Most High? Every bit was true and made perfect sense. I was supposed to be the one nurturing and caring for the baby primarily. Despite the remnants of feminism still lingering in my soul, I knew it was right.

It is okay to acknowledge that women by design are nurturers. God created us to birth and care for babies, not our husbands. And it is okay to accept that. It is necessary to accept that. It brings peace to your heart and your family when you accept that.

As soon as my son popped out, I felt I knew what he needed and knew how to hold him. I felt a drive in my being to care for him despite being exhausted from labor. As God spoke, not only did I carry the baby for almost a year, my body actually produced food for the child. If we pay attention to creation and how God made and designed things, we can observe His intentions for His creation. Many things become quite clear.

A father has a very important role in a child's life, and of course he should be as helpful and supportive as he can as his wife nurtures the babies. But in those early years of the child's development, a mother's love, and acceptance of her place as nurturer is of the utmost importance.

If a family struggles financially, the bulk of that pressure will fall on the husband. Provider is his role, designed by God. If we look at the Creator's design, we will be free from a lot of confusion when it comes to so many things, including the order of family.

1 Timothy 2:15

Notwithstanding she shall be saved in child-bearing, if they continue in faith and charity and holiness with sobriety.

Titus 2:3–5

The aged women likewise, that they be in behaviour as becometh holiness, not false accusers, not given to much wine, teachers of good things;

That they may teach the young women to be sober, to love their husbands, to love their children,

To be discreet, chaste, keepers at home, good, obedient to their own husbands, that the word of God be not blasphemed.

PRAYER

Abba Father, thank you for your patience love and guidance. Your wisdom is mighty, you have created all things. God, I humble myself to you and receive the role of motherhood as a gift.

You created my body to bear children. This is your doing, and it is good. Lord, give me grace to fulfill this role well, fully accepting in my heart the order you have set through creation. In the Mighty name of your son, Yeshua I pray. Amen.

Speak Life Into Your Family

*Speak life over yourself, your marriage, and family even
when things are a mess and seem to be falling apart.*

The word of God brings life and purpose. If we are in Christ, God
has blessed our families with purpose. Speak life over yourself, your
marriage, and family even when things are a mess and seem to be
falling apart.

The purpose God gives our lives is so important and helps make
us who we are. External circumstances do not change the purpose
and calling we have as individuals or collectively as a family.

Focusing on who each person is and what God has called them
to do will help you value them as people, instead of thinking about
the negative. Seeing the purpose that you have as a family will help
bring value to each person in the family, instead of making the things
that support the family (the house, furniture, yard, activities, aca-
demics) the main focus.

If you are able to speak words of life and have joy and peace
when things are less than perfect, then you will see those things spoken by the Lord come to pass. If you wait for things to get perfect
before you believe, you will never walk in the FULLNESS of God's
promises.

You have to tell your child who they are and who God has called
them to be when they are throwing tantrums and misbehaving. You

have to tell your child who they are and who God has called them to be when they are having self-esteem problems. You have to speak life and tell your child who they are when their grades are failing.

YOU HAVE TO SPEAK LIFE and God's purpose over your family. That is part of being a builder and building your house.

Another important fact to remember, you are part of the family, and need to be on the list of people to love and care for. Speak life over yourself also, Sis! Your spiritual, emotional, mental, and physical health are important. Taking care of yourself positions you to be able to care for the needs of others from a place of wholeness.

Speak God's word over yourself, over your mind, body and spirit man. Speak God's promises over yourself, your marriage, and your family, even if things are not perfect right now. This will encourage and strengthen you, instead of letting negative thoughts overtake you when things are not going well.

God's word is alive, and speaking it brings life to bodies, purposes, marriages, families, situations, and circumstances!

Proverbs 18:21

Death and life are in the power of the tongue: and they that love it shall eat the fruit thereof.

1 Peter 3:10

For he that will love life, and see good days, let him refrain his tongue from evil, and his lips that they speak no guile:

2 Corinthians 10:14

We having the same spirit of faith, according as it is written, I believed, and therefore have I spoken; we also believe, and therefore speak;

PRAYER

Abba Father, you are clearly seen in the things you have made. Your glory, majesty and wisdom are undeniable. Lord, you have created me in your image, and you have given me the ability to speak life with my mouth.

God let joyfulness be in my heart and a river of life flow from my mouth towards my family. God, I want to be a wise woman and build my house and speak life over my family. Please show me how to do this and give me grace. Lead me to scriptures to pray for my children and household. In the name of your son, Yeshua I pray. Amen!

Find A Friend

Two is better than one.

If you have safe babysitting, go out by yourself, and hang out with other Godly women regularly. Or have frequent play dates with other Godly families who encourage, inspire, and build you up!

This principle has been so vital for my family and me. Since I had my first baby, I realized my need to be in fellowship with other Godly women. I have done many things to meet this need.

Everyone is busy so it can be tough to align schedules, however it is worth the effort. Ask an older Godly woman you look up to out to lunch or ask another mom with children close in age with yours if she would like to meet up for a playdate at a park. You can plan a ladies' night out for several Godly girlfriends to get together. Inviting a family over for dinner is another great way to have fellowship.

You can do a combination of things. Set a goal of doing something to meet and fellowship with another Godly woman once per month. Seeing people at church is great, but there is not always time for meaningful conversation after or between big church services. So be intentional.

Over the years, I have had so many great conversations, and learned so many things, and have been encouraged in so many ways just from fellowshipping with other women.

There have been periods when my family and I were going through very difficult times and fellowshipping over dinner with another Godly family greatly lifted our spirits. Sharing stories, testimonies, advice, discussing the word, dreams, and visions, laughing; these moments can be transformative.

Perhaps you do not have a lot of friends in Christ. Maybe you don't have big pool of moms that you can pick from to hang with or an older woman to encourage you. The bible says, if you want friends, show yourself friendly! You initiate the interaction!

Pray and ask the Lord to send Godly women in your life that you can learn from and be built up by, and when you sense Him presenting the opportunity, don't be shy!

Proverbs 27:9

Ointment and perfume rejoice the heart: so doth the sweetness of a man's friend by hearty counsel.

Proverbs 27: 17

Iron sharpeneth iron; so a man sharpeneth the countenance of his friend.

PRAYER

Abba Father, I thank you for the wisdom in your word concerning friendship. I thank you for the Godly friends I have now, and I pray that you would surround me even the more with Godly women who I can do life with and bear fruit with.

Father God, please deliver me from all ungodly friendships and fruitless relationships in my life.

I pray that you would help me to encourage younger women to love their husbands and children, and I pray that you would send older Godly women to encourage me. Lord, help me to be a Godly mother who bears Godly fruit in my children's lives in the name of your son Yeshua I pray. Amen.

Strengthen Your Heart

If you want a peaceful home, you have to have a peaceful heart.

There are so many voices, thoughts, and things that we subconsciously judge ourselves against. It is very important for us as mothers to silence negative voices in our minds. If you want a peaceful home, you need to have a peaceful heart.

Some people have more of a natural tendency to be overly critical of themselves. What we hear, or the voices we allow to prevail in our hearts have a direct effect on our emotions and how we feel about ourselves and our families. Critical thoughts are the thief of peace.

Social media is the icing on the cake of negative thoughts. Moms posting their best moments, the high accomplishments of their children, and perfect pics of their perfect homes. Oh yes, and how perfect their bodies are just weeks after giving birth!

We have access into each other's lives in a way that has never been possible at any other time in history. However, what is "posted" on social media is not always reality, rather a snapshot of time, sometimes artificially staged. We are left coveting a life, family or body that may not even be real.

As servants of the Most High, we are called to examine ourselves, we are called to love the truth and not lie to ourselves.

> *James 3:14 But if ye have bitter envying and strife in your hearts, glory not, and lie not against the truth.*

It is a Godly thing to evaluate yourself and see if you are walking in God's truth in your life.

> *1 Peter 1:22 Seeing ye have purified your souls in obeying the truth through the Spirit unto unfeigned love of the brethren, see that ye love one another with a pure heart fervently:*

God wants us to look at ourselves honestly and ask for help overcoming any ungodliness that we know is in our hearts and life.

However, we are also called to encourage ourselves! Celebrate your victories, feel good when you get it right! Pray and ask for help when you fail.

Balance is very important. You do not want to pretend like you do not see the deficits in your Christ-like character, nor do you want get so discouraged that you give up every time you make a mistake.

Too much negativity only discourages us and makes us feel like we can never change. Dis-COURAGE-ment steals courage from us. It steals the courage that we need to fight and win. Discouragement steals courage that we need to speak God's word and steals the courage that we need to forcefully take the victory that Christ died to give us.

> *Philippians 4:8*
>
> *Finally, brethren, whatsoever things are true, whatsoever things are honest, whatsoever things are just, whatsoever things are pure, whatsoever things are lovely, whatsoever things*

are of good report; if there be any virtue, and if there be any praise, think on these things.

Romans 15:13

Now the God of hope fill you with all joy and peace in believing, that ye may abound in hope, through the power of the Holy Ghost.

2 Corinthians 13:11

Finally, brethren, farewell. Be perfect, be of good comfort, be of one mind, live in peace; and the God of love and peace shall be with you.

PRAYER

Abba Father, thank you for your patience with me. Please help me to have peace in my heart. Help me Lord God to think on good things, on whatever is true, honest, just, pure, lovely and of good report. God, I cannot do this without your anointing, help, and strength.

Please give me your peace on the inside, so I can model peace to me family on the outside. Help us to overcome negativity, critical thoughts, and hurtful words. Jesus, you came to give me peace, and as your disciple I receive it in the name of your son, Yeshua I pray. Amen.

Order is a Precious Gift

Order in our homes is one of the greatest gifts we can give our children.

The order of the family is: Christ as the head of man, man as the head of woman, and children obeying their parents in the Lord.

If we can live this in our homes, it will help set an example for our children and future generations of our families.

> **1 Corinthians 11:3**
>
> **But I would have you know, that the head of every man is Christ; and the head of the woman is the man; and the head of Christ is God.**
>
> **Ephesians 6:1**
>
> **Children, obey your parents in the Lord: for this is right.**

After the wedding, there is a spiritual attack launched against the union. If the enemy can convince the husband to not love His wife as God commanded, he knows he has a chance at breaking up that marriage covenant.

If the enemy can get the wife to be disobedient and disrespectful to her husband, the enemy knows he has a chance at breaking up that marriage covenant.

Well, that attack set in early in our marriage. I remember before I got married, I fully agreed with the man being the head, and I was very convinced that God's order was best for families. However, once I got married, it was a lot harder to live out than read about.

People say that marriage is a mirror, and it shows you who you really are. That was definitely true in my case. After we were married, it was very difficult for me to submit to my husband.

I was very self-willed and felt the need to express my opinions on almost every decision he made. To be honest with you women of God reading this, I had a spirit of Jezebel and I did not know it. Jezebel was a foreign woman who married an Israelite King named Ahab. She introduced idolatry to God's people, usurped authority over her husband, and threatened to kill the prophets of God. You can read about her wickedness in the books of first and second Kings.

The root of Jezebel is rebellion against God's order. I felt that as long as I was not arguing with him, I could politely state my opinions when I needed to. However, women are called to submit to their husbands, not overrule his authority with their own opinions.

Submission means that you take on the mission of that person, not with lip service but in your heart. I was so used to making my own decisions. But looking back I recalled glimpses of this issue in my childhood as well, having trouble submitting to my parents.

God has been merciful to me in teaching and showing me my errors and through His grace I have repented. We are currently praying and working to establish God's order and authority in every area of our family.

There have been some difficult days, but His Word is our daily bread and eating all of it, transforms us from the inside out. Our Father has great blessings for us when we seek to eat all His word, Saints. Be encouraged to serve God in your family, be encouraged to submit to your husband, even as he grows in his leadership and decision making.

PRAYER

Abba Father, please help me to submit to you as I submit to my husband. Please forgive me for ways that I have failed at being respectful, obedient, and submitted to my husband. God, I want to grow and set a good example for my children.

Please give me power to become the servant of God, wife and mother that you want me to be. Please help my husband become the Godly leader of our home that you want him to be. Please strengthen him in areas he is weak and help him to submit to you as his head and leader. Father, I want your order in my home. In the name of your son, Yeshua I pray. Amen.

Final Thoughts

Motherhood has been greatly devalued in our society. Through media, the feminist movement, abortion indoctrination, and the pursuit of our so-called "best life", women are sent a message: to value other careers and a life of leisure above being a mother.

Even within my own soul, I struggle to see the value of motherhood. Daily, I cast down thoughts that I am wasting my youth raising children. This a lie which stems from the lust of the flesh, lust of the eyes, and the pride of life. We live in a culture that values youth, beauty, and sexual attractiveness, and pride more than wisdom, fruitfulness, or servanthood.

In the age of abortion on demand and a host of contraceptives to ward off pregnancy, human life is seen as expendable. When motherhood became a choice, the heart became more unsettled with the difficulty of motherhood. Why did I choose this? I should have chosen something else. Reality is that motherhood is one of the most important jobs on the face of the earth. The Lord tells us to be fruitful and multiply and replenish the earth. The Bible tells us that children are a reward from the Lord. The Bible tells us that having lots of children is a blessing, not a curse.

Our values are backwards, friends. Right has become wrong in our eyes. What God calls a blessing now feels like a curse in our hearts that long for autonomy more than we want to give Him the Godly seed that He has asked for.

As women of God, it is time for us to recalibrate our desires. Do we really love what God loves? Do we really hate what he hates? He loves fruitfulness, he says children ARE a blessing.

Are we able to bring our thoughts under subjection to God's word? That is the only way to have any measure of lasting success. Not success by society's standards, but eternal success.

When I was a new mother and my oldest child was only a few months old, my husband and I were running a house of prayer in Detroit for 40 days. The hours were 6:00 p.m.–12:00 a.m. daily. It was at one of the prayer meetings that the Lord showed me what I now call the Anointing of Motherhood. In prayer, the Lord broke through to my spirit and revealed to me that the church must receive an anointing for motherhood and fatherhood to contend against the spirit of abortion. We cannot pray for God to end abortion in America, while Christian couples continually reject children via contraception. God's solution to abortion, violence, and the death culture is Godly motherhood.

If the word of God says that children are a blessing (Psalms 127), and that one of the purposes of marriage is because God seeks godly seed (Malachi 2); yet we as Christians reject those blessings, we are being disobedient to God's command to be fruitful and multiply. Disobedience is as the sin of witchcraft (1 Sam. 15:23).

In order to take authority over the issue of abortion, we have to obey and receive God's word in this area and let our minds be renewed about the purpose of children and family. We cannot condemn the world of aborting babies, then go in the bathroom and swallow birth control pills. We have created the term "family planning" which sounds nice, but what is birth control? Attempting to control the birth of children (when, how many, how far between). Wait, isn't that God's job?

From Jochebed (Moses' mother) to Hannah (Samuel's mother) to Elizabeth (John the Baptist's mother) and Mary (Jesus's mother), God has always brought His people deliverance through the Anointing of Motherhood.

There are some women that face serious health challenges that make childbearing life threatening. My heart goes out to families who face these kinds of issues. Truly Yah can show women with health concerns their unique path to motherhood and how He wants them to have an impact on the next generation, be it having children, adopting, fostering, or mentoring.

I can testify that raising small children is difficult. Young parents need the help, support, and guidance of the elders as the Bible states. Older women truly teaching younger women would help relieve a lot of the stress and pressure that make some Christians not want to have many children (but that is another topic).

However, if we return to the biblical view of the purpose of family, it would dramatically change our view and we would find that we have the grace to raise however many children the Lord gives us, whether biological, adopted, or foster.

I pray that we would all approach the task of motherhood with joy, and look forward to watching our seeds of love, patience and hope grow up in our babies, who will grow into the next generation of Godly fathers and kind mothers.

Good News for You! The Gospel of Salvation Through Jesus Christ:

The most important aspect of motherhood is leading your children to God, and the only way for you to do that is if you are following God also. Having a relationship with the One who created you is the most important relationship possible.

The reason that He wants to help you is because eventually, He will have to judge you. Here is what will you be judged for:

1. **You will be judged for your WORDS:**

   Matthew 12:36 But I say unto you, That EVERY IDLE WORD that men shall speak, they shall give account thereof in the day of judgment.

   37 For BY THY WORDS thou shalt be JUSTIFIED, and BY THY WORDS thou shalt be CONDEMNED.

2. **You will be judged for your ACTIONS:**

   Revelation 2:19 I know THY WORKS, and charity, and service, and faith, and thy patience, and thy works; and the last to be more than the first.

   Revelation 3:2 Be watchful, and strengthen the things which remain, that are ready to die: for I have not found THY WORKS perfect before God.

   Revelation 20:12 And I saw the dead, the great and the small, standing before the throne, and books were opened; and another book was opened, which is the book of life; and the dead were JUDGED from the things which were written in the books, ACCORDING TO THEIR DEEDS.

2 Corinthians 5:10 For we must all appear before the JUDGMENT seat of Christ, so that each one may be RECOMPENSED for his DEEDS IN THE BODY, according to what he HAS DONE, whether GOOD or BAD.

3. **You will be judged for the TRUTH you HEARD but REJECTED and IGNORED:**

Matthew 12:47 And if any man HEAR MY WORDS, and BELIEVE NOT, I judge him not: for I came not to judge the world, but to save the world.

48 He that REJECTETH me, and RECEIVETH NOT MY WORDS, hath one that judgeth him: THE WORD THAT I HAVE SPOKEN, the same SHALL JUDGE HIM IN THE LAST DAYS.

This info on EXACTLY what we will be JUDGED ON comes DIRECTLY from Jesus the King and Judge of all of Us!

But the Good News is that He offers forgiveness, healing, and deliverance for you if you repent from sin and obey Him.

More Good News is that He not only tells us what we will be JUDGED by, He tells us EXACTLY HOW TO PASS THE TEST OF JUDGEMENT!

HERE IS HOW YOU CAN PASS YOUR JUDGEMENT DAY TEST:

1. Repent to God: TURN AWAY from your sinful ways and thoughts, and Keep God's 10 Commandments.
2. Believe in and Obey Jesus the King: The Son of God's death, burial, and resurrection gave you the opportunity to get FORGIVENESS and SALVATION from your sins.
3. Get Baptized in Water: For your NEW LIFE and your new beginning.

4. Pray for an overflow of the Holy Spirit and receive the POWER TO OBEY God, demonstrate, and tell others everything you have seen and heard about Jesus.
5. Be taught and DISCIPLED in the Scriptures.
6. CONNECT with a commandment keeping assembly of believers.
7. LISTEN to God's Voice and OBEY God daily.

If you would like to connect with our ministry in real life or receive free Kingdom discipleship training, go to <u>*www.h2h2hop.com*</u>